STRONG MEN SERIES STU

THE CLIMB

BOOK 2:
FIGHTING APATHY

JIM RAMOS

COPYRIGHT

DEDICATION

I'm especially grateful for our number one champion- Shanna. Her amazing faithfulness and relentless trust have literally changed my life. She is my hero.

The Climb is dedicated to the myriad of men and women who have championed the cause of Men in the Arena. We are fighting an uphill battle to transform lives through teams of men.

Our vision is way beyond any one man or ministry. I'm so grateful to all who have captained teams, given financially, prayed faithfully, served administratively, and offered their wisdom, expertise, and leadership.

TEAM CAPTAIN RESOURCES

You've received The Strong Men Series at a conference, from our website, your pastor, or possibly a friend. Now what? If you're holding this book, then you are a magnum enough man to figure it out on your own. This book is dangerous and has the power to change lives because within its pages are reference after reference from the Book of books.

You may still have some questions; we know this. We've provided several resources to help you on your journey to transform the lives of men and those they love, because when a man gets it—everyone wins.

First, check out our website (www.meninthearena.org). There you will find tons of great resources designed to inspire and equip you towards your best version.

Second, join thousands of men from around the world on our exciting Men in the Arena closed Facebook forum for men. Engage with men every day as they dialogue about what a man is and does. Do you need more help? We have a team of Arena Coaches ready to help you!

Third, subscribe to our wildly popular Men in the Arena Podcast. The Men in the Arena Podcast targets men living in the "Stress Bubble of Life" who are hardworking, loving one wife, raising godly children, and serving in their community.

Fourth, check out the QR Code before each meeting that links to an introductory video. Each video will help guide you to the best meeting possible.

SEND US A PICTURE OF YOUR TEAM

SEND US A PICTURE OF YOUR TEAM AND YOUR HERO STORY

We have no way of knowing who our resources are impacting, but we'd love to celebrate with you. Send us a picture of your team. We'll post it on social media and in our monthly newsletter if the photo is high quality and we have space.

Also, send us your stories of transformation that we call Hero Stories. God is the famous one, but He has chosen you to be the hero for your family. When a man gets it—everyone wins. If we happen to share your story, we will shoot you some swag to say, "Thanks!"

When you send the team picture, let us know where you're from (city, state, and/or country), who the leaders are, and where you meet (coffee shop, living room, church, etc.). Thank you for partnering with us.

INTRODUCTION

Who may ascend the mountain of the Lord?
Who may stand in his holy place?
The one who has clean hands and a pure heart,
who does not trust in an idol or swear by a false god.
Psalm 24:3-4

"Slow and steady. Slow and steady."

Big Darby whispered these words of encouragement between breaths as we climbed the sheer face with packs weighed down by the New Mexico mule deer I shot. I'm not sure if his words were meant to encourage me or self-talk himself up the mountain.

But it worked.

Similarly, I once asked my father-in-law how he marched for so many miles with such heavy pack loads during his Marine days, and his response was simply, "Slow and steady. Slow and steady."

If hope and anticipation characterize the trailhead, then pain and resistance describe the climb. In fact, a man is ignorant at the trailhead exactly once. Afterward he knows what to expect. If the pain is too great or resistance too strong, he may never climb again.

But pain and resistance are part of the climb. They're part of life. They're a part of being a man. Temptation to quit is the test of pain. Quitting however, is not an option when ascending the mountain of manhood. Yet too many men fall victim to attrition on the steep slopes of manhood, leaving the lives of those they love littered along the way by a male who couldn't transition to man.

Every male is anatomically similar, but not every male is a man. The world is filled with males who saw the looming climb and chose the low road instead of pushing through the pain and resistance towards the top.

Others sadly, begin the climb, but can't hack it. They drop their responsibilities along the path like some overloaded pack that belonged to someone else. Like Everest carcasses from days gone by, all passers-by see the carnage of his cowardly decision to remain a boy.

Manhood is tough. The fight against apathy is the greatest battle a man will ever fight. It's the most difficult mountain a man will ever climb. Like the author of Hebrews, any man who's completed the journey to the summit will admonish younger men to train hard and pack light.

"Let us throw off everything that hinders and the sin that so easily entangles. And let us run with perseverance the race marked out for us"
Hebrews 12:1

I love it!

To climb is to fight resistance. This takes passion, strength, and perseverance. Failing to battle the forces that weigh us down results in apathy, weakness, and attrition. Apathy is simply a loss of feeling. The Bible calls this callousness. Calluses form when something loses its ability to resist friction, as seen on the hardened hands of a construction worker.

But when a man refuses to resist the forces that press against him, the callus forms over his heart. He becomes indifferent to the causes and people he should care deeply about. He becomes hardened and unfeeling. He becomes calloused. A defining moment comes when a man wakes up in the morning, looks in the mirror, and decides to fight the forces trying to push him down and commits, once again, to climb the mountain of manhood one painful step at a time.

Slow and steady.

Manhood is a hill worth dying on and a life worth living. Slow and steady.

Slow and steady.

Welcome to The Climb.

A WORD FROM THE AUTHOR

Welcome to the multimedia edition of the Strong Men Study Series. In this new edition we've added QR codes at the beginning of each chapter. You can scan the QR codes with your smartphone or tablet to access all team meeting introductory videos.

In these videos we introduce you to the content of each study. These brief presentations are designed to prepare your mind and heart for each team study.

At the end of the book you'll see a page called, "New Team Launch Steps" with QR codes leading up to your Men in the Arena team launch. The videos are a great resource for any man desiring to launch a new team. We emphatically recommend that every man partner with another man, to eventually start his own team. You've got this!

There are many QR readers available for smartphones and tablets. Check your device. It may already have one installed. Thank you so much for championing the cause of Christ on behalf of men because when a man gets it—everyone wins.
Jim Ramos

TABLE OF CONTENTS

TEAM MEETING ONE: CALLOUSED

> *"I want to ride to the ridge where the west commences. I can't look at hobbles and I can't stand fences. Don't fence me in."*
> *"Don't Fence Me In"* ~ Cole Porter

Welcome to The Climb!

Welcome to the second book of five in the Strong Men Study Series-The Climb. Apathy is a man's greatest fight. We live in a world of calloused, indifferent, passive men. Tragically, many have succumbed to society's emasculating voices telling them to defer their God-given responsibility to lead. But those voices are liars.

Fight against them. The Climb is strategically designed to help men win the war against apathy. Like climbing a steep mountain, apathy is defeated one step at a time, one day at a time.

Here's Webster's Definition of apathy.
1: Lack of feeling or emotion: impassiveness. 2: Lack of interest or concern: indifference. Origin of apathy: Greek apatheia, from apathēs without feeling. First known use: 1594.

This book is appropriately titled, The Climb: Fighting Apathy. When you read this, why do you think this topic is so important?

Check out this story. A high school English teacher was going over the definition of words with her students and asked, "What is the difference between ignorance and apathy?" One bored young man leaned over to his equally disengaged buddy and whispered, "I don't know, and I don't care!"

TEAM MEETING AT A GLANCE

- Opening Prayer, Weekly Announcements
- Personal and Victory Stories
- Each man will share his story—one man per week until all men have shared.
- After all men have shared their personal story, allow time each week for them to share victory stories.
- Weekly Study Closing Prayer
- Closing Prayer

> *"This world's so full of emptiness, bringing me down. And I'm so tired of feeding my senses, draining me out."*
> *"Savior Divine" by Something like Silas*

Like the young man in the story, when does apathy manifest a just-don't- care-anymore attitude in your life?

What are the long-term effects of this kind of attitude?

Who suffers the most because of it?

Read Matthew 13:13-15 and similar passages Isaiah 6:8-10 and Acts 28:23-28.

This is why I speak to them in parables: "Though seeing, they do not see; though hearing, they do not hear or understand. In them is fulfilled the prophecy of Isaiah: "'You will be ever hearing but never understanding; you will be ever seeing but never perceiving. For this people's heart has become calloused; they hardly hear with their ears, and they have closed their eyes. Otherwise they might see with their eyes, hear with their ears, understand with their hearts and turn, and I would heal them.'"
Matthew 13:13-15

Written over 700 years before Christ, Isaiah 6:1-13 is titled "Isaiah's Commission." Jesus quotes the Isaiah passage in Matthew 13:1-23 in the "The Parable of the Sower". Years later in Acts 28:17-31, The Apostle Paul addresses Jewish leaders at Rome in a section titled, "Paul Preaches at Rome Under Guard".

In Matthew 13:15 Jesus quotes Isaiah, "For this people's heart has become calloused; they hardly hear with their ears, and they have closed their eyes." How do calluses form?

Illustration: Gloves are worn to protect the hands from blisters. Blisters result from constant friction. Gloves prevent friction by creating a protective layer close to the hands. Gloves maintain the sensitivity in the hands by fighting the resistance the tool would otherwise create. Without gloves the friction created between the worker's tool and hands eventually forms a blister. Blisters, over time and constant friction, evolve into calluses in order to protect the hands. The hands eventually became callused – hard, tough, and unfeeling.

For the worker, calluses are a good thing, a protective layer helping him work longer hours. What are the dangers of a calloused heart?

A calloused heart doesn't happen overnight. The heart hardens over time. Let's look at two warning signs of apathy.

First, is the ability to hear God speak, "They hardly hear with their ears".

Think about this. What habitual voices eventually damage your ability to hear God?
Isaiah 30:21, Proverbs 3:5-6, Romans 12:1-2, and Galatians 5:22-25. The loss of hearing is the result of failure to protect my ears over time – it's habitual.

For example: If I refuse to wear hearing protection while shooting guns, I eventually suffer hearing damage due to the passivity (habitual neglect) over time.

Second, how is hardly hearing different than closing your eyes?
"And they have closed their eyes".
Matthew 5:8 and Ephesians 1:17-19

"You cannot judge what you do not know about me against what you do know about yourself."
~Mike Yaconelli

Illustration:Wild animals are more vulnerable to predation when two or more of their protective senses (sight, smell, or hearing) are removed. Hearing loss occurs over time due to passivity (habitual neglect) but closing the eyes is a decisive choice. When I close my eyes I'm deciding to not see something. When I close my eyes to God (and His Word) I'm openly defying Him.

When are you most tempted to close your eyes to God's truth?
Matthew 6:13, Romans 3:23, 6:23, and James 1:13-15.

In Matthew 13:14-15 Jesus offers a way to cut away the callouses by turning back to Him; "Otherwise they might see with their eyes, hear with their ears, understand with their hearts and turn, and I would heal them." Where do you need to turn?
2 Corinthians 7:9-11, and 2 Timothy 2:24-26

Where, towards whom, has your heart hardened—become calloused and apathetic?

Break into groups of three or four.

Take a moment today and pray for each other.

> *"The bed of sloth often proves the bed of lust."*
> ~John Wesley

STUDY NOTES

For the next five days, read the following entries from our **The Field Guide: A Bathroom Book for Men.**

We hope they challenge and encourage you to get in the great Arena for God. See you on the Arena Floor!

CONFRONT THE MOUNTAIN

Impossibilities vanish when a man and his God confront a mountain.
~Abraham Lincoln

While on a hunt in Southern Oregon I befriended a man named Martin who lived in our campground. Square-jawed and built like an NFL linebacker, he was a hurting man who loved the Bible and a book called, God's Little Devotional Book for Men.

Psalm 91:4 was part of his daily reading ritual, "He will cover you with His pinions, and under His wings you may seek refuge; His faithfulness is a shield and a bulwark." (NASB)

As I pondered Psalm 91:4, I felt an overwhelming sense that God wanted me to give him my most expensive hunting jacket. Over breakfast in our motorhome I shared his life verse and presented him with the jacket. He tried it on.

Perfect fit! With tears streaming down his chiseled jaw he embraced me with a new understanding of Psalm 91:4. God "will cover you."

The next day he forced me to accept a worn copy of his devotional book. Today's quote was found there. The mountains seem to grow the older we get. The aging man tends to lose the youthful enthusiasm of the climb and avoids the steep slopes. Mountains appear insurmountable, so we take the detour instead. We learn to climb smart, not hard. We ignore the painful invitation of the mountain.

Instead, confront the mountain. Confront the muddy secrets bogging down your life. Confront the gluttonous avalanches smothering your vitality. Confront the rolling hills that have softened you. Confront the cliffs of fear that have trapped you in mediocrity. Confront the mudslide of disobedience to God's Word. Confront the mountain and discover that God is faithful and will cover you.

NEVER DOUBT

Sometimes wrong, never in doubt.
~Philip Wirth

After a quarter of a century of vocational youth ministry, I resigned my Youth Pastor position to pursue a full-time role as the Founder and President of Men in the Arena. Our vision is to "transform lives through teams of men". The weight of raising enough money to support our fledgling organization, as well as my family, rested upon my shoulders.

Shanna and I made the five-hour drive to a small one-horse town in Eastern Oregon to visit our friend Phil and get some desperately needed advice.

Friends call Phil "The Rhino" because he charges forward in everything he does. He's a country boy who believes his big God has called him to push back darkness through his uncanny ability to develop Kingdom resources.

As I shared my heart-pounding tension between anxiety and faith he stopped me mid-sentence. "Lately, I use a phrase that helps me. I believe God has called me to do certain things, so I live by the words, 'Sometimes wrong, never in doubt.'"

Never doubt what God is saying even if you're wrong in how you go about it. Charge forward with unwavering faith.

A week later another man spoke Romans 4:20 into my life. It's the story of Abraham leaning into God's promises, "With respect to the promise of God, he did not waver in unbelief but grew strong in faith, giving glory to God" (NASB).

He did not waver. He did not doubt. He simply said, "Yes." What has God placed on your heart?

You already know the answer, don't you? Then pursue it with diligence. Pursue it with a rhino-like passion. Break down the walls of fear and uncertainty.

Sometimes wrong, never in doubt.

ME TIME

However, I consider my life worth nothing to me, if only I may finish the race
and complete the task the Lord Jesus has given me—the task of testifying
to the gospel of God's grace.
Acts 20:24

I once spoke to a male who hunted and fished three days a week. His addiction to hobbies ultimately cost him his family. During a grueling stretch of at least four days of work in a row he whined, "I need me time!"

He lost a godly woman and sons over his me time. This male misunderstood that manhood is more about we time than me time. Anatomically he was male but, at forty, had yet to act like a man. He abandoned his marriage covenant for fish. What do you think he taught his sons through his abandonment?

He was confused.

In Acts 20:24 Paul affirms his call to "testify of the Gospel of God's grace." To Paul, finishing meant more than ending. It was to "complete the task the Lord Jesus has given me."

A male sacrifices his family for "Me Time." A man surrenders his wants for the needs of others as if saying, "I consider my life worth nothing to me." He'll put me time aside in order to embrace his responsibility in leading those who depend on him. Simply, a man knows that "we" is more important than me.

What is your life worth to you compared to those you love? You say you'll take a bullet for them?

How about now?

NO HESITATION

*"My procrastination, which had held me back, was born out of fear
and now I recognize this secret mined from the depths of all courageous hearts.
Now I know that to conquer fear I must always act without hesitation
and the flutters in my heart will vanish."*
~Og Mandino
The Greatest Salesman in the World

In the summer of 2000, I climbed Mt. Whitney in a day. Mt. Whitney is the tallest mountain in the contiguous United States at 14,497 feet. It's ironic since I'm not a fan of heights. I remember a PE teacher coercing me to jump off the high dive as I hesitantly inched my way to the edge of the board. After ten minutes of mock jumping and begging for reprieve, I took the horrible plunge.

I walked the plank.

I prefer my feet secure on the ground, thank you very much. I can climb any wall, tree, or high ropes course if securely fastened. Remove that security and I'm convinced a leap of faith is a leap to death.

That high dive experience reinforced what I believed about the relationship between fear and hesitation. The longer we stand on the edge, the more difficult it is to jump. I agree with what John Eldredge states in his book Wild at Heart that every man has an "adventure to live".

Adventures are lived by jumping in without hesitation, with both feet, without dangling our toes in the water.

What if Peter hesitated to walk on water (Matthew 14:28-29)? What if David feared the size of Goliath (1 Samuel 17:17-51)? What if Paul wanted empirical evidence regarding the source of the blinding light (Acts 9:1-27)? What if Moses searched for a route around the Red Sea (Exodus 14:10-16)?

They all would have been anonymous in the pages of His-story.

Life is too short to hesitate. Jump!

INSANE HABITS

"Insanity is doing the same things over and over but expecting different results."
~ George Patton

My friend Doug plants his field with corn or millet every year. Salt Creek runs along the field and floods after a hard rain making it the perfect habitat for ducks. Each year Doug invites a select group of men to hunt on his property. On one crisp January morning my son Darby and I sat in the gray dawn listening to literally thousands of ducks landing on the water. It was a surreal experience.

Joy turned to frustration, however, as I soon discovered I couldn't hit anything. I shot without adjusting my swing and, of course, continued missing. I burned through a box of shells before finally making an adjustment. That change made all the difference. If I'd only made it sooner.

Actions over time form habits. I've battled bad habits all of my adult life. The secret to a life fully alive is breaking the habits that bring death or darkness, while forming habits that bring life and light.

Make your adjustments sooner rather than later. Don't expect different results when banging away at life, praying, but never changing. When you keep missing the target, evaluate your life. Is there any habitual sin that you're hiding? Are you openly rejecting what God has asked you to do? Who is locking arms with you in your journey?

Then act.

Measure the distance between who you are and who God wants you to be. Chart a course of personal growth. Build proper habits and make the right adjustments in order to hit the moving target we call life.

TEAM MEETING TWO:
SLOW FADE

"From time to time you will be tempted to compromise your character for the sake of expediency. Resist. Maintain your moral authority. Your moral authority is what makes you a leader worth following. Abandon the vision before you abandon your moral authority."
~Andy Stanley, Visioneering

What did you take away from last week's study and daily readings? What are you still processing? What challenged your current paradigm? What inspired you to grow as a man?

Calluses are formed over time. They disappear just as slowly unless they're ripped off suddenly. When sin is uncovered (before confession and repentance) the collateral damage and public humiliation can be devastating. The once hidden sin is ripped wide open and put on public display. When have you witnessed this firsthand?

Today we are studying the story of David and Bathsheba (2 Samuel 11:1-12:31). David will be our guide through sin, shame, repentance, and restoration. There is hope of restoration for those who have had their calluses ripped away, being exposed in sin.

We hope this encourages those caught in sin, that there is light at the end of the tunnel. Let this serve as a warning however, for those living in secret sin. Repent now before those you love become collateral damage in the wake of your sin.

How is David remembered? What phrase is often used to describe his relationship with God?
1 Samuel 13:11-14 and Acts 13:21-22.

TEAM MEETING AT A GLANCE

- Opening Prayer, Weekly Announcements
- Personal and Victory Stories
- Each man will share his story—one man per week until all men have shared.
- After all men have shared their personal story, allow time each week for them to share victory stories.
- Weekly Study Closing Prayer
- Closing Prayer

> *"This Psalm (51) is often and fitly called 'The Sinner's Guide.' In some of its versions, it often helps the returning sinner. Athanasius recommends to some Christians, to whom he was writing, to repeat it when they awake at night. All evangelical churches are familiar with it. This is the first Psalm in which we have the word Spirit used in application to the Holy Ghost."*
> ~William S. Plumer

What caused David to descend into adultery, deception, and murder? Better yet, how did he ascend out of sin to be known as "man after God's heart"?

The story of David's sin with Bathsheba and the murder of her husband Uriah the Hittite (one of David's Mighty Men) is found in 2 Samuel 11:1 to 12:9. Turn there now.

The entire city of David occupied no more than ten acres.
The Holman Bible Dictionary

What do the Proverbs teach us about pride?
Proverbs 8:13, 11:2, 13:10 16:18, and 29:23

"Springtime, which marks the end of the rainy season in the Middle East, assures that roads will be in good condition (or at least passable), that there will be plenty of fodder for war horses and pack animals, and that an army on the march will be able to raid the fields for food. Every able-bodied man in Israel went to war—except the king. The contrast between David and his men could hardly be expressed in starker terms. Staying home in such situations was not his usual practice. Leading one's troops into battle was expected to be the major external activity of an ancient Near Eastern ruler."
~Commentary Critical and Explanatory on the Whole Bible

In 2 Samuel 11:1-3 we see boredom trigger David's lust and voyeurism (modern day porn). What triggers your lust?
Proverbs 6:6-9, 20:4, 21:25, Matthew 5:28, Colossians 3:5, and 2 Samuel 12:1-9

"The Hebrews, like other Orientals, rose at daybreak, and always took a nap during the heat of the day. Afterwards they lounged in the cool of the evening on their flat-roofed terraces. It is probable that David had ascended to enjoy the open-air refreshment earlier than usual. Perhaps because of the oppressive heat of a spring sirocco, David lengthens his afternoon siesta into the cooler part of the day. Getting up from his bed and taking a stroll, from the roof of his palace he sees a 'very beautiful' woman bathing. The heat of the unusually warm spring day has forced the woman to bathe outside to escape the suffocating hot atmosphere of her house."
~Commentary Critical and Explanatory on the Whole Bible

In 2 Samuel 11:4 coveting and selfishness manifest themselves in full-blown adultery. How would you describe the progressive nature of the lust?
Exodus 20:17, Matthew 5:27-28, 1 Corinthians 6:18-19, and 1 Thessalonians 4:2-4

David digs a deeper hole of sin in 2 Samuel 11:4-12. How does the web of sin create more lies to hide the darkness?
Galatians 6:6-8, 1 Timothy 1:10, and Revelation 21:8

How does drunkenness (2 Samuel 11:13) medicate something much deeper?
Ephesians 5:18, 1 Peter 4:3, Proverbs 23:21, Romans 13:13, 1 Corinthians 5:11, and Galatians 5:21

In 2 Samuel 11:14-27 we see David deteriorate into murder and outright evil. How does a man fall so far?
Exodus 20:13, Isaiah 59:7, Matthew 5:21-22, Romans 1:29, 6:23, and James 4:1-2

"Some men are more predisposed to passive thinking, and it's not rocket science to figure out why: fear and related emotions like anxiety have too much influence over them. We don't respect passive people any more than we like aggressive people. The goal is to become assertive."
~Paul Coughlin
No More Christian Nice Guy

Read how David's secret sins are eventually exposed in 2 Samuel 12:1-11. What can we learn about David's heart (and sin's deceptive power) from his response?
2 Samuel 12:13.

What is the difference between the shame of sin and repentance from sin?

Let's take a look at David's repentance as he guides us through the process described in Psalm 51.

> *"The superscription relates the context of the Psalm (51) to David's heinous sin with Bathsheba, after David had been rebuked by the prophet Nathan. The lament form of the Psalm suitably fits the spirit of contrition and prayer for restoration. Gone are the questions. What remains is a soul deeply aware of sin, of having offended God, and of its desperate need of God's grace."*
> ~The Expositor's Bible Commentary

The integrity of the upright guides them, but the unfaithful are destroyed by their duplicity. Wealth is worthless in the day of wrath, but righteousness delivers from death. The righteousness of the blameless makes their paths straight, but the wicked are brought down by their own wickedness. The righteousness of the upright delivers them, but the unfaithful are trapped by evil desires. Hopes placed in mortals die with them; all the promise of[a] their power comes to nothing. The righteous person is rescued from trouble, and it falls on the wicked instead.
Proverbs 11:3-8

> *"There is no other Psalm which is oftener sung or prayed in the church."*
> ~Martin Luther *on Psalm 51*

Discuss each of the steps mapped out in the Psalm 51, known as the "Sinner's Guide".

The subtitle of Psalm 51 is, "A psalm of David. When the prophet Nathan came to him after David had committed adultery with Bathsheba."

- Admission of sin (Psalm 51:1)
- Believing in forgiveness of sin (Psalm 51:2)
- Confession of actual sin (Psalm 51:3-4)
- Acknowledging our default to sin (Psalm 51:5)
- Acknowledging that sin is a choice (Psalm 51:6)
- God's forgiving power (Psalm 51:7-9)
- God's redemptive power (Psalm 51:10-12)
- God's deliverance power (Psalm 51:13-15)
- Restoration of a humble heart (Psalm 51:16-17)

As bad as it might seem, God is in the business of restoration for those willing to follow the Sinner's Guide to repentance. What can we learn about the heart of God from 2 Samuel 12:24-25?

Compare 2 Samuel 12:26-29 with 2 Samuel 11:1.

What did David learn through it all?

You may have a tremendous heart for God. How will you insure yourself to keep that heart for Him? What warnings do you gather from David's life?

Confession is a manly trait.

Break into groups of three or four.

Is there any secret sin that you'd like to confess and repent of?

Take a moment today and pray for each other.

> *"The redemptive power of God is seen in the birth of Solomon, who would not only be known as the wisest man to ever walk the earth, but was also in the lineage of the Messiah."*
>
> ~Jim Ramos

STUDY NOTES

For the next five days, read the following entries from our **The Field Guide: A Bathroom Book for Men.**

We hope they challenge and encourage you to get in the great Arena for God. See you on the Arena Floor!

DO WORK

*"I firmly believe that any man's finest hour, his greatest fulfillment in all he holds dear,
is the moment when he's worked his heart out in a good cause
and lies exhausted on the field of battle—victorious."*
~Vince Lombardi

Who could forget the opening scene in the movie Saving Private Ryan, of D-Day (June 6, 1944) when allied troops invaded France! The opening scene shows US soldiers unloaded and many slaughtered by German machines guns as amphibious Higgins boats unloaded them onto Omaha Beach to fight or die.

This scene is a classic representation of the "death ground" described in Sun Tzu's book, The Art of War. Death ground is simply when leaders place their men in a fight or die situation. Men are wired to fight.

We're born to climb the hill we may die on. Without that bloody hill, that place to fight, a man wanders into the valley of apathy—a death of a different kind. I'll never forget when my oldest son James returned from working out in the weight room, flexed and said, "Dad, I did work today."

We're living in one of the worst economies in American history. Thousands of men have lost their jobs and are in danger of wandering aimlessly without purpose, focal point, and venue to "do work." But work doesn't define the man. God does. Our work is to serve the King, "Whatever you do, work at it with all your heart, as working for the Lord, not for men" (Colossians 3:23).

Baseball legend, Yogi Berra once said, "When you come to the fork in the road, take it!" This is good advice for wandering men. Find a hill, any hill, and climb it. Just move. Like Moses, shout to the Lord, "Now show me your glory!" (Exodus 33:18).

Once you start moving that fighting spirit will return. Take the fork in the road even if you're unsure. God will guide you as you put one foot in front of the other.

WILD MEN

Let us fix our eyes on Jesus, the author and perfector of our faith, who for the joy set before him endured the cross, scorning its shame, and sat down at the right hand of the throne of God.
Hebrews 12:2

January is welcomed with open arms as a new beginning. January is a breath of fresh air after the gluttony of the holidays. January is a second chance that, God willing, arrives every twelve months.

It's also a time to seek God's will in the coming year. Along with new goals, I choose a focused theme or mantra for the next twelve months. The theme unleashes something wild inside—a new challenge.

The propensity of life is to domesticate a man's wild spirit. The monotony of life tames the wild man inside of us. We need more. We need to unleash the wild man. We need something that unleashes him in us.

Even the Church tries to domesticate a man, to tame him, so he won't be too offensive. I have nothing against being domesticated; unless, of course, you're a man. Domesticated and emasculated aren't too far apart and neither one is any way to go through life. Wouldn't you agree?

Scottish philosopher, Thomas Carlyle (December 4, 1795 - February 5, 1881) said, "Every noble crown on this earth is, and will forever be a crown of thorns."

It's much easier to be domestic than a barbarian. In his book, Wild at Heart, John Eldredge writes, "Every man has a battle to fight". A barbarian without a battle will soon be feeding chickens. Barbarians aren't welcome today. They're unrefined. They're intimidating.

Return to your barbarian roots. Pick up the crown of thorns. Press it firmly onto your scalp, and carry the cross up the hill you may die on.

BEAR THE YOKE

The Lord is good to those whose hope is in him, to the one who seeks him; it is good to wait quietly for the salvation of the Lord. It is good for a man to bear the yoke while he is young.
Lamentations 3:25-27

Cardiovascular exercise came easier when I was a younger man than it does now. The difference between the twenties and forties is about one pound per year, which is a literal burden I carry daily. The burden of added weight is not what I would call a good yoke!

The word "good" is mentioned three times in today's passage. Good can be defined as something that agrees with one's concepts and opinions. It's favorable or virtuous. But, the word "good" in Hebrew means something quite different.

According to the Expositor's Bible Commentary, good means, "That which expresses God's will and purposes." In other words, it is God's will "for a man to bear the yoke while he is young."

It's good to learn the disciplines necessary to carry the weight of manhood as a young man. It's good for children to be under the discipline of parents (Hebrews 12:7-11) because it's in the foundational years of childhood that he learns to become a man.

In his youth a man's habits are formed, morals solidified, and his God is chosen. A man becomes a man as a boy. Conversely, a boy remains a boy even if he is physically a man.

Chronological age does not turn a male into a man — the choice to transition from male to man does. Carry the weight while you are young so you don't have to carry it when you're older.

Learn to be a man sooner rather than later.

BATTLEFIELD SACRIFICE

So give your servant a discerning heart to govern your people and to distinguish between right and wrong. For who is able to govern this great people of yours?
1 Kings 3:9

For it is commendable if a man bears up under the pain of unjust suffering because he is conscious of God.
1 Peter 2:19

In a 1962 speech to cadets at the US Army Military Academy, General Douglas MacArthur said:

"The soldier, above all other men, is required to practice the greatest act of religious training — sacrifice. In battle and in the face of danger and death, he discloses those divine attributes, which his Maker gave when he created man in his own image. No physical courage and no brute instinct can take the place of the Divine help, which alone can sustain him.

However horrible the incidents of war may be, the soldier who is called upon to offer and to give his life for his country, is the noblest development of mankind…the soldier above all other people prays for peace, for he must suffer and bear the deepest wounds and scars of war. But always in our ears ring the ominous words of Plato, that wisest of all philosophers: 'Only the dead have seen the end of war."

Just as the soldier battles the unjust tyrannies of this world, a man battles on behalf of his wife and children. He's often the first to wake and the last to bed. Statistically, he's the first to die as well. A man willingly sacrifices his life for those he loves.

Men can take it, because we are men.

We can take it because Jesus took one for the team on the cross. We can take the pain because we are "conscious of God". We can handle struggles on the battlefield of life. Men are the walking wounded of families. A man proudly makes the necessary sacrifice for the family he loves so much.

PRE-GAME VICTORY

Be strong and courageous. Do not be afraid or discouraged because of the king of Assyria and the vast army with him, for there is a greater power with us than with him.
2 Chronicles 32:7

Years ago, my son's youth football team finished undefeated. As coaches we'd watch the other team during warm-ups to see if they'd show us their hand. Prior to the championship game our opponents ran a play we'd never seen before.

I told our defensive end what to do in that formation and, sure enough, when they ran their special play we picked it off, ultimately winning the game. Their coach was shocked that we stopped his secret play and when he asked about it I told him we watched him running it before the game.

This young coach learned a valuable lesson that day. As Bill Hybels said, "Everything rises and falls on leadership." We often see teams stuck in the basement rise to the top of their division by something as simple as a coaching change. A great coach knows how to lead men.

Today's passage is a message to Hezekiah from God. Hezekiah was recognized in history because of his faithfulness to God. He was a spiritual leader that people could trust. Hezekiah trusted that God wouldn't send him into a battle he couldn't win.

We win some and we lose some.

But God's plan is for us to win. Victory is ours when we move in God's will, and in God's timing. When God calls us to new battlefields, He not only blesses, but goes before us into battle!

I don't know about you, but I want God to fight for me, not against me. I want God to scout out the territory He wants us to conquer. Don't move before or after Him.

Move with Him.

TEAM MEETING THREE:
DEALING WITH PMS

"You miss 100% of the shots you never take."
~Wayne Gretzky

What did you take away from last week's study and daily readings? What are you still processing? What challenged your current paradigm? What inspired you to grow as a man?

PMS isn't what you think. Our goal is to deconstruct traditional views dealing with this ailment. Where do you struggle with PMS (Passive Male Syndrome)?

You are a male. But are you a man? Why is the word "male" used instead of the word "man" in PMS? How is a male different than a man? How is he similar?

In Genesis 3:1 we read, "Now the serpent was more crafty than any of the wild animals the Lord God had made. He said to the woman…" Being "more crafty," why did he speak to Eve instead of Adam?

The ordinary man is passive. Be extraordinary.

Where do you think Adam was during the dialogue between Eve and the Serpent?
Genesis 3:6-7

The passive man is pathetically anonymous in his own story.

32

TEAM MEETING AT A GLANCE

- Opening Prayer, Weekly Announcements
- Personal and Victory Stories
- Each man will share his story—one man per week until all men have shared.
- After all men have shared their personal story, allow time each week for them to share victory stories.
- Weekly Study Closing Prayer
- Closing Prayer

> *"I'm convinced, after counseling hundreds of couples for more than two decades, that a major factor in the failure of marriages is the passivity of men."*
> ~Bill Perkins
> *Six Battles Every Man Must Win*

Discuss the possibilities why Satan addressed Eve and not Adam.

Possibility 1: Satan knew he could not engage Adam in a war of words. It's debated that men use an average 10-15 thousand words a day, but women use a whopping 20-30 thousand. When a man comes home from a long day of work, his wife is just warming up!

Possibility 2: Generally, men are literal in their interpretations of words. Women are much more interpretive.
Example: When your wife asks if you'll drive her car to the store, you'd better come home with the gas tank filled!

Possibility 3: While clearly present when Eve ate the fruit, Adam may not have been around for the dialogue with Satan.

Possibility 4: God's authority to lead was on Adam, but Satan loves causing division and confusion. 1 Corinthians 14:33, Revelation 12:10

Possibility 5: Adam may have been too busy staring at Eve's naked body to hear the dialogue between Eve and the Serpent!

Possibility 6: Adam sat passively by (Genesis 3:6-7) and Eve dialogues with the Serpent

> *"The ordinary man is passive...against major events, he is as helpless as against the elements. So far from endeavoring to influence the future, he simply lies down and lets things happen to him."*
> ~George Orwell

"Suddenly, he stopped and stared. He had never seen the creature who stood before him. In a way, she looked like him. But she also looked different— beautifully different. After years alone, without a companion with whom to talk, laugh, dream, hold, and make love, Adam finally beheld his match—the crown of God's creation. She was flawless: physically, mentally, and spiritually. She possessed every attribute Adam could ever want in a lover and friend. And she carried no baggage from her past. No corrosive bitterness, ugly scars, crippling regrets, or selfish expectations (or belly button). She had no stain, she was without par."
~Bill Perkins
Why Naked Women Look So Good

Discuss Bill Perkins' quote. Who is to blame in the Garden?
Romans 5:12-14 and 1 Corinthians 15:20-22

The passive man is soft and has no spiritual punch. What is Eve's responsibility in the Garden?
1 Timothy 2:11-15

The consequences of PMS are devastating!
Genesis 2:24-25, 3:6-7, and 21-22

"As naturally aggressive as Adam was, when the moment of authentic manhood arrived-when he was called upon to act responsibly, take charge spiritually, and protect his woman—Adam just stood there! He went flat. He became passive. He refused to accept the social and spiritual responsibilities entrusted to him by God. Men have been imitating Adam... ever since. Real manhood begins with a decision to reject social and spiritual passivity when nothing is the more comfortable and natural option."
~Robert Lewis
Raising a Modern Day Knight

Adam and Eve fell from being naked before God (and each other) with "no shame" to covering their nakedness with fig leaves. Adam's passivity reduced the prototypical man to a male desperately sewing fig leaves to hide his nakedness from his wife—the only other human on the planet!

Sin kills. Where did the "garment of skin" (21) come from? Why did something have to die?
Romans 5:6-8, 6:23, 1 Corinthians 15:3-4, 2 Corinthians 5:14-17, and Hebrews 9:15.

How is PMS killing those around you?

Who is suffering because of your PMS?

"Passive men extend something that looks like grace—a disposition to be generous, helpful, and merciful. However, the reason passive men accept insults and other forms of humiliation is that they fear what might happen with an eruption of conflict—the sound of life happening."
~Paul Coughlin
No More Christian Nice Guy

Break into groups of three or four.

Where are you most passive?

Take a moment today and pray for each other.

STUDY NOTES

_____

_____

_____

_____

_____

_____

_____

_____

_____

_____

_____

_____

For the next five days, read the following entries from our **The Field Guide: A Bathroom Book for Men.**

We hope they challenge and encourage you to get in the great Arena for God. See you on the Arena Floor!

TRY NOT TO LOSE

Be strong, Philistines! Be men, or you will be subject to the Hebrews,
as they have been to you. Be men, and fight!
1 Samuel 4:9

When it came to choosing which football scholarship to accept, a winning football program was non-negotiable. I'd become comfortable with losing at a high school that recorded a dismal ten wins, and one tie, out of thirty varsity football games. Sadly, I'd come to expect losing.

I'd forgotten who I was. I'd forgotten how to win. I'd forgotten how to compete, and it scared me. The fight to win was lost and competition was reduced to playing not to lose.

Focus on not missing the shot and you miss.

Focus on not saying the wrong thing and you say it.

Focus on not failing and you fail. You'll hit the object of your focus, win or lose, good or bad.

Focus on the win. It's what you were made for.

In today's passage, the men of Israel brought the Ark of the Covenant to the battle lines as a source of encouragement. Then, "all Israel raised such a great shout that the ground shook"
(1 Samuel 4:5).

The Philistines were instantly intimidated. The temptation to not lose had set in. Knowing the odds were stacked against them, they decided to "take courage, and be men." They could've walked away with their lives but chose to be men and fight, and probably die. But they fought courageously and won.

Does it really matter what the odds are, or what we think the outcome might be? All that matters is that we, as men, fight and are willing to die for what we believe.

What do you believe in with such conviction that you'll win or die to achieve?

MIND FIELD

For though we live in the world, we do not wage war as the world does.
The weapons we fight with are not the weapons of the world. On the contrary, they have divine power
to demolish strongholds. We demolish arguments and every pretension that sets itself up against the
knowledge of God, and we take captive every thought to make it obedient to Christ. And we will be
ready to punish every act of disobedience, once your obedience is complete.
2 Corinthians 10:3-6

At a recent health screening I found my blood pressure was high and blood sugar levels unhealthy. Since childhood I've had eating problems, snacking at midnight almost every night since I can remember. Today's passage speaks to my current state of health. Today is a motivator to get back up and fight the battle over personal sin.

God gives us spiritual weapons to "demolish strongholds." Weapons such as those listed in Ephesians 6:10-18 need to be used often. God's men use their Bibles, including memorization, prayer, fasting, and practicing accountability.

Spiritual weapons are anything that connects us to God's diving power. Spiritual weapons are used to destroy each and every thought that separates us from God. Our weapons are also used to, "take captive every thought to make it obedient to Christ."

For example, my current health issues are diet-related. Diet-related issues are, for the most part, thought-related issues. Simply put, my mind is in bondage to food. Food owns me. I struggle to resist it.

Spiritually, this is a huge problem.

Thoughts that aren't contained weaken mind, body, and spirit. Whether it's to food, drink, laziness, lust, or greed: the Word of God offers wisdom to live by. No temptation is too great for a man to hold captive.

Take captive any thoughts that captivate you.

GO WITH THE FLOW

But the people refused to listen to Samuel. "No!" they said. "We want a king over us. Then we will
be like all the other nations, with a king to lead us and to go out before us and fight our battles."
1 Samuel 8:19-20

Chuck Swindoll in Living Above the Level of Mediocrity wrote, "The majority is usually wrong." Swindoll admonishes readers to follow Jesus, make their own choices, and choose to swim against the current.

One of the greatest struggles of our time is the fight against popular culture. God strategically placed us in the world but doesn't want us to be polluted by it (Philippians 4:8). If we're going to be in error while following Christ let it be on the side of Christ not culture, the minority not majority, and against the current rather than with it.

"But everybody's doing it!"

The majority is usually wrong. Israel wanted to go with the flow. They wanted a King. Israel wanted to "be like all the nations." Worse, they chose to follow a man to "go out before us and fight our battles."

Did I read that right?

They abolished their God-centered government, exchanging it for a human king. They decided to go with the majority instead of having the courage to possess their uniqueness as a nation.

Many claim to follow Jesus, but live according to popular culture. They listen to the media more than the Word of God. They trust their pastor instead of God. They celebrate their church more than their salvation. They pursue the earthly things instead of the eternal.

They're going with the flow.

Don't be that man. Swim upstream.

Fight the majority view. Fight the apathy it creates.

YOUR GOLIATH

David said to Saul, "Let no one lose heart on account of this Philistine; your servant will go and fight him."
1 Samuel 17:32

Ground shrinkage is a term describing when a hunter convinces himself that the animal in his scope is larger than life. Most wish for a great trophy but will settle for something much less. Settling happens when high-powered scopes convince a hunter the animal in sights is larger than he really is. We squeeze the trigger only to be disappointed when up close.

Goliath was a giant figuratively and literally. He towered over the men of Israel while raining down intimidating threats and cursing God. For forty days the men of Israel cowered in his presence.

Goliath was also a figurative representation of the giant of disbelief among the Israelite warriors. David saw the giant of unbelief and remembered past victories over lesser giants. He picked up five polished stones and the rest is history.

But why did he pick up five stones and not one if he had such great faith? The short answer is, who cares? But if you need to know, here's why. David had a win or die attitude. That loudmouth giant was going down. David knew one of the stones in his hand would be the one to do it.

Interestingly, David presented King Saul with the giant's head, but kept the armor for himself, I believe, as a symbol of his victory over unbelief. It marked a milestone in his life as a man who could take down giants.

Kill the giants in your life.

Have you identified them? If so, keep throwing stones until the giant of unbelief falls.

STRANGE FEAR

Be strong and let us fight bravely for our people and the cities of our God. The Lord will do what is good in his sight.
2 Samuel 10:12

The most dangerous thing about hunting in the Western Oregon mountains are the dark-timbered forests. Moving to Oregon I soon discovered how easy it was to get turned around in the dark timber. I tried to avoid it, but learned you often have to drop into these dark and brushy canyons to find success. My fear, based on inexperience, temporarily froze my efforts.

As David sent the best men of Israel to fight the Ammonites and Arameans, he noticed they were outnumbered and surrounded. The situation looked bad for David's men until they heard the courageous statement found in today's passage.

Courage comes when we're under fire.

Courage is fear confronted. Courage is fear defeated. There's no courage without fear lurking close by. Courage is not the absence of fear, but victory over it. Just as the fear of dark timber froze me, courage drops into the deep canyons of the unknown in spite of fear.

Victory aligns with our fears when we trust in God's faithfulness. One of the greatest battles to fight is the battle over fear. Fear can either paralyze a man or motivate him. Fear can cause a man to pick up five stones and fight or cause him to hide behind a rock. Fear keeps us on the ridgeline. Courage drops into the dark timber.

What fears have paralyzed your faith and life lately?

Where do you need to act in courage over something that's paralyzed you in fear?

TEAM MEETING FOUR:
THE WALKING DEAD

"I wish more people would have the guts to stand against the passivity that is choking the life out of Christian men."
~Paul Coughlin
No More Christian Nice Guy

What did you take away from last week's study and daily readings? What are you still processing? What challenged your current paradigm? What inspired you to grow as a man?

Today we're going to dream big. Each of us will have the chance to share. You were given twenty-five thousand dollars, and one week to do whatever you wanted with the only stipulations being: 1) you had to do it with friends, 2) you had to spend all the money, and 3) it had to be something that fueled your fire. What would it be?

Today's lesson is all about discovering (or rediscovering) your passion. What are some dangers in living dangerously? What are some of the dangers in rediscovering your passions in life?

The popular book by Rick Warren, Purpose Driven Life lists several categories that make up your spiritual S.H.A.P.E. The "H" represents your heart or passion. In other words, pursuing your passion is a pathway to spiritual vitality and discovering who you are.

Compare the creation of Adam in Genesis 2:5-9 to the creation of Eve in verses 2:18-25. Can you see any differences and how they might be significant in addressing a man's desire for adventure?

TEAM MEETING AT A GLANCE

- Opening Prayer, Weekly Announcements
- Personal and Victory Stories
- Each man will share his story—one man per week until all men have shared.
- After all men have shared their personal story, allow time each week for them to share victory stories.
- Weekly Study Closing Prayer
- Closing Prayer

> *Adventure, with its requisite danger and wildness, is a deeply spiritual longing written into the soul of man. Every man has an adventure to live."*
> ~John Eldredge
> *Wild at Heart*

"Eve was created within the lush beauty of Eden's garden. But Adam, if you'll remember, was created outside the garden, in the wilderness. Man was born in the outback, from the untamed part of creation. Only afterward is he brought into Eden. And ever since then boys have never been at home in the indoors, and men have had an insatiable desire to explore. We long to return; it's when most men come alive."
~John Eldredge
Wild at Heart

Is the desire for the wild side, the adventurous life, from God or is it something men fabricate? Explain.

God wired a Sabbath rest into our lives to renew our strength and fuel our passion for life.

When does pursuing your passions, become unhealthy and childish?

When our renewing passions violate our biblical mandate, we've crossed back over from men to male. Check out Jesus' words in John 10:10b.

What role does adventure play when men live the "full life"?

The Greek word for life is zoe. Zoe speaks of the life that is given by God through Christ Jesus to those who believe the gospel. It means life eternal, everlasting, of endless duration. In other words, it refers to life that starts the moment a man receives Jesus and continues through eternity. It's literally eternal life starting now!

What threatens to rob men of their ability to live the full life? Why do so many good men surrender the full for the mundane life?

"Men living in the stress bubble (aka "The Arena") of raising a family walk on the razor's edge of responsibility and renewal. Where is the balance between leading responsibility and living adventurously?

> *"The attitude of so many Christian (men) today is anything but fierce. We're passive, acquiescent. We're acting as if the battle is over, as if the world and the lamb are now fast friends."*
> ~John Eldredge
> *Waking the Dead*

What lessons would you like to share with the younger men? What can we learn from men who have traveled before us?

Before he was released into public ministry, Jesus was led by the Spirit into the wilderness. Why the wilderness? What role (if any) does the wilderness play in wrestling with God?
Matthew 4:1-11 and Luke 4:1-13

Take a look at another wild man, John the Baptist. What made him so wild?
Luke 3:1-6 and 7:24-25

Where (what place) do you go when you wrestle the most with God?

Read the account of Jacob. When was the last time you wrestled with God? Where did you go?
Genesis 32:9-12 and 32:22-31

> *"When a man comes to the mountains he comes home."*
> ~John Muir

> *"Every man dies. Not every man truly lives."*
> ~Braveheart

What lessons would you like to share with the younger men? What can we learn from men who have traveled before us?

Before he was released into public ministry, Jesus was led by the Spirit into the wilderness. Why the wilderness? What role (if any) does the wilderness play in wrestling with God?
Matthew 4:1-11 and Luke 4:1-13

Take a look at another wild man, John the Baptist. What made him so wild?
Luke 3:1-6 and 7:24-25

Where (what place) do you go when you wrestle the most with God?

Read the account of Jacob. When was the last time you wrestled with God? Where did you go?
Genesis 32:9-12 and 32:22-31

"We need men who refuse to let biology define their destiny and who live inspired by a fiery inner vision of the masculine life."
Steven Mansfield

> *"The only difference between a rut and the grave is the size of the hole."*
> ~Unknown

What do these passages stir inside of you? Does the promise of persecution fire you up, frighten you, or both? Explain.
Matthew 10:16-23 and 2 Timothy 3:12

Where do you need God to disturb the monotony (of your life) and rekindle your passion for adventure?

Disturb us, Oh Lord, for the things that disturb you! Wake us up! Shake us up!
Break us up for the things that break your heart.

"What makes life difficult isn't that we experience pain. It's made difficult by our passivity, which undermines our willingness to fight through pain."
~Bill Perkins
Six Battles Every Man Must Win

Where to you need to rediscover yourself?

Break into groups of three or four.

Where do you need to recommit to something you were once deeply passionate about but lost along life's way?

Take a moment to pray for each other.

STUDY NOTES

_____

_____

_____

_____

_____

_____

_____

_____

_____

_____

_____

_____

_____

For the next five days, read the following entries from our **The Field Guide: A Bathroom Book for Men.**

We hope they challenge and encourage you to get in the great Arena for God. See you on the Arena Floor!

KING OF THE JUNGLE

Choose the best and most worthy of your master's sons and set him on his father's throne. Then fight for your master's house.
2 Kings 10:3

In California we called them mountain lions. Other places call them pumas. Most Oregonians call them cougars. These shy and highly elusive animals strike fear in the hearts of men without ever being seen. Hunters carry pistols, walk only during the daylight, and are keenly aware of their surroundings when they enter lion country.

Although dangerous, these animals fear man and are rarely seen in the wild. In fact, in over four decades spent in the outdoors, I've only seen one mountain lion.

On that particular outing, we went to sleep about 300 yards from where a lion was last seen. That angry cat kept us up all night screaming murderous threats of malcontent at our presence. We'd ventured into the lion's territory and were in danger of becoming the prey instead of predator.

In Revelation 5:5, Jesus is referred to as the "Lion of Judah". Maybe that's why C.S. Lewis chose the Christ-figure, Aslan, to be a lion in his Chronicles of Narnia series. Maybe it's because of what a lion is capable of. Maybe it's because lions don't back down. Possibly it's because the elegant adult male's mane resembles a crown.

Who knows?

The man who follows Jesus is the son of "The Lion of Judah" and an heir of the King. We're at the top of the food chain as long as we live in the Lion's country. Like the lion, a man should never back down. He knows who he is and where he comes from.

You are a son of the King of the jungle.

Act like it.

Live like it.

Love like it

STALLING

God is with us; he is our leader. His priests with their trumpets will sound the battle cry against you. Men of Israel, do not fight against the Lord, the God of your fathers, for you will not succeed.
2 Chronicles 13:12

Have you ever been in a fight you knew you couldn't win? Here's one that stands out from my past. In my junior year of high school our varsity basketball team had seven players, one senior, and no one over six feet tall.

We actually practiced a Stall Offense to keep the stacked St. Joseph High to less than one hundred points. We knew we had no chance against a team with three players taller than six feet, six inches.

It didn't work. They scored 100 points easily.

How refreshing it is to know that followers of Jesus don't have to stall. We're the ones who win big. Why then, do we cower when it comes to sharing Jesus with friends, family, and co-workers? We boast of inviting someone to church and cower when inviting them to Jesus. If we know we're on the winning team then why live small?

Live with the confidence of the winners we are. Live like the champions God created. Live large. Stand up. Get in the game instead of sitting on the bench. Lead the charge to victory.

I wonder what message a coach sends his athletes by stalling from the first possession. Yes, we got spanked that night. Yes, we would've been beaten ninety-nine out of one hundred times. But isn't that one chance at victory worth going hard for, even if the other ninety-nine are losses?

Would you fight hard if you knew you might win? What if you knew you would?

Will you fight or stall?

Get in the ring. Fight!

PINTO COVENANT

Be strong and let us fight bravely for our people and the cities of our God. The Lord will do what is good in his sight.
1 Chronicles 19:13 (NASB)

As young boys, my brother and I were riding bikes to the local market on a candy quest. I got caught in the middle of a yellow light and was hit by a yellow Ford Pinto. Thankfully, I was uninjured, except for a few scratches. How much damage can a Pinto do?

I limped my wounded Schwinn home and tried to calm my brother, who witnessed the event, while thinking of something to tell my parents. I ended up bribing Tom with my only quarter. He kept that secret for over forty years. It was the covenant of one brother to another.

In this passage we see a covenant made between Joab and his brother Abshai. Surrounded by the enemy, Joab and Abshai made a covenant to come to the aid of the other and Joab sealed the deal with the inspirational words "Be strong and let us show ourselves courageous for the sake of our people and the cities of our God; and may the Lord do what is good in His sight" (NASB).

The New International Version of the Bible says, "Let us fight bravely." In our soft culture that neuters men, being a man takes strength.

Strength is tested through resistance. Resistance comes to those who fight for what they believe is true. Fighting bravely is fighting with the covenant to win or die fighting. This kind of courage originates with covenant. It's the promise made between a man, his God, and the men who lock arms with him in life's battle.

Who are your men in battle? Who do you consider family? Who is your band of brothers?

Who needs to know that you have their back?

CELEBRATING FOUL BALLS

I have fought the good fight, I have finished the race, I have kept the faith.
2 Timothy 4:7

When my son James started playing baseball he was the smallest guy on the team. His early at-bats were painful to watch as he either struck out or walked every time he stepped to the plate. I thought he'd want to quit. Instead, he begged me to help him improve.

We bought a makeshift backstop and practiced every day at hitting an old tire, then to the batting tee, and finally hitting tosses. He slowly improved, the next game, hitting two foul balls before striking out. It was time for a celebration!

The next game, he hit a single and scored two runs. By the end of the season he was awarded The Most Improved Player of the team. I was so proud of his courage and tenacity. He absolutely refused to give up.

Quitters are everywhere these days. We quit our jobs, quit our families, quit our marriages, and quit our faith. Fewer men seem to be serious about their faith. But faith is a good thing. In fact, Paul calls it the "good fight" in several places in Scripture (1 Timothy 1:18, 6:12, 2 Timothy 4:7).

Faith is worth fighting for.

Nothing good comes to a man who is handed life on a silver platter. Parents who spoil their children are hurting them. Life demands a fighting effort. But it's easier to be passive and entitled than to fight. The passive man waits for the pastor or church to somehow help him. It won't happen.

But the assertive man takes faith by the horns and does something about it. He takes action and initiative. While the passive pray for God's will the assertive are busy living boldly.

To claim to "have finished the race", means you've "kept the faith", and resolved to "fight the good fight" until the final breath.

BACKPACKS

Therefore, since we are surrounded by such a great cloud of witnesses, let us throw off everything that hinders and the sin that so easily entangles, and let us run with perseverance the race marked out for us.
Hebrews 12:1

I'm a strategic thinker. Doing research, analyzing contingencies, and developing or figuring out the best play energizes me. My friend, "Big" Darby is different. Problem solving energizes him. He loves to fix things, which makes us a great team because I usually break things. Essentially, I look at problems from the outside-in while Darby sees them from the inside-out.

Our backpacks are a perfect example of this. My pack is methodically organized with every item strategically positioned before I step out of the truck. Darby starts tossing things into the pack at the trailhead, and never stops adjusting his pack.

I smile in disbelief as Darby searches for something else he's lost somewhere in the bottom of his pack. In New Mexico, he had so much extra gear lashed to the outside that the pack extended sideways four feet. It destroyed a lot of innocent brush that day.

He refused to "throw off " what potentially "hindered" him and created more work.

I regularly advise men to lighten their load. Often they choose to ignore my counsel and carry extra baggage such as hidden sin, pursuits of pleasure, and guardrail-violating relationships. How you live out your faith is your choice. Realize, however, that the choices you make have collateral damage if they're the wrong ones.

The race of faith is a weighty enough challenge without the extra baggage. It's ridiculous to walk "entangled" with added burdens. (Galatians 6:1-2).

What's in your pack? What unnecessary baggage are you hauling? Who are you carrying with your bitterness? What sins are you hiking with?

TEAM MEETING FIVE:
LOST AND FOUND

"To see the world, things dangerous to come to, to see behind walls, draw closer, to find each other, and to feel. That's the purpose of life."
~The Secret Life of Walter Mitty

What did you take away from last week's study and daily readings? What are you still processing? What challenged your current paradigm? What inspired you to grow as a man?

Life has a way of robbing us of the dreams and pleasures of youth. Life has a way of unwinding. But Jesus came to give us life the full. It's time to reclaim what we've surrendered and live again.

Where has life seemed to have stolen something from you? Reflecting on your life, have you lost yourself somewhere along the way?

What are you asking God for? What does He need to find for you?

"It was fitting to celebrate and be glad, for your brother was dead, and is alive; he was lost, and is found."
Luke 15:32

Take turns reading "The Healing at the Pool" story in John 5:1-15.

The pool is called Bethesda, which in Aramaic means "house of mercy." This name is symbolic of what's about to happen.

Verses 5-7 offer some insight into this man's possible state of mind. What other information can we gather?
Matthew 9:27, 15:22, 17:15, and 20:30-31

54

TEAM MEETING AT A GLANCE

- Opening Prayer, Weekly Announcements
- Personal and Victory Stories
- Each man will share his story—one man per week until all men have shared.
- After all men have shared their personal story, allow time each week for them to share victory stories.
- Weekly Study Closing Prayer
- Closing Prayer

> *"Instead of praying 'If I die before a wake'*
> *we should pray 'If I wake before I die.'"*
> ~Mark Driscoll

The missing verse (4) from The Healing Pool Story reads: "for an angel of the Lord went down at certain seasons into the pool and stirred up the water; whoever then first, after the stirring up of the water, stepped in was made well from whatever disease with which he was afflicted" (New American Standard Bible).

This verse is missing in many translations. If you use the New American Standard Bible or New Century Version you will see the verse, but it's been placed inside brackets, whereas the King James Version and the New King James Version contain verse four without any notation or demarcation. Verse four isn't found in manuscripts dated prior to the fourth century and most accurate manuscripts of the Gospel of John.

This suggests that verse four doesn't belong in the New Testament, which explains why many modern Bible translations omitted it.

How does the invalid's answer reflect his victim mindset? How is this mindset passivity in disguise?
Romans 12:1-2, Philippians 4:6-8, Hebrews 12:1-2, and 2 Corinthians 10:5

> *"Disturb us, Lord, to dare more boldly, to venture on wider seas where storms will show your mastery, where losing sight of land we shall find the stars."*
> ~Sir Francis Drake

The Climb is subtitled, Fighting Apathy. Fighting apathy is a battle against the forces trying to keep men static, passive, and motionless by the pool. Gravity is a negative force when climbing a mountain and must be overcome in pressing towards the summit. Fighting apathy is a mindset leading to action: it's boots on the ground not poolside philosophies. Apathy may be the greatest fight a man will ever battle.

How does Jesus respond to this mindset in verse 8-9? How might Jesus' response be similar to the passive man of today?

In John 5:9b-12 the paralytic seems to have felt no particular gratitude to Jesus for his healing. He took no responsibility for his healing on the Sabbath. After Jesus dealt with him the second time (14), he quickly informed the Jewish leaders that Jesus was the Sabbath violator they were looking for.

In more ways than one this man was lost. Even after being healed by Jesus his mindset didn't change. Jesus' mindset is much different. In verse 14 we read, "Later Jesus found him at the temple and said to him, 'See, you are well again. Stop sinning or something worse may happen to you."

Why would Jesus go to such an effort to find this man?
Jesus does not ignore passivity.

What does this tell you about God's view of PMS (Passive Male Syndrome)?
PMS was the cause of man's fall in the Garden of Eden and Jesus being raised on the cross.

What did Jesus mean when He said, "See, you are well again. Stop sinning or something worse may happen to you"(14)?

Imagine five years from the healing. What does this man's life look like? How can helping someone become enabling?

How does this story speak to the apathy of modern man? How does it speak about you?

> *"Give a man a fish, feed him for a day. Teach him how to fish, feed him for a lifetime."*
> ~Unknown

Break into groups of three or four.

What area(s) of your life need to be assertively "found" by you?

Take a moment today and pray for each other.

> *"Men need to bark at the moon. Men need to blow something up. Men need to push themselves into a zone they don't control—that in fact isn't actually a zone. Men need to go in pursuit. They need a quest."*
> ~Steven Mansfield
> *Mansfield's Book of Manly Men*

STUDY NOTES

_____

_____

_____

_____

_____

_____

_____

_____

_____

_____

_____

_____

_____

For the next five days, read the following entries from our **The Field Guide: A Bathroom Book for Men.**

We hope they challenge and encourage you to get in the great Arena for God. See you on the Arena Floor!

RUN AT IT

Should a man like me run away?
Nehemiah 6:11

Never forget an extra inner tube or patch kit when riding a mountain bike. A flat tire, ten miles from the truck, without the tools to fix it, makes for a long walk back. Trust me, I know.

Similarly, there are many snags along life's trails that tempt to deflate us.

For example, it's easy to walk away during the childrearing years in The Stress Bubble — to go flat. It's even easier to make excuses in a world with already low expectations for men.

Today's passage challenges our temptation to go flat—to walk away from commitments. Nehemiah's response to death threats is an inspiration for every man. Nehemiah understood that running to the temple would be running away from his leadership responsibilities (Nehemiah 6:10).

Because he was a pillar of hope for the Jews, his enemies were highly motivated to deflate, and ultimately remove him. Instead of running, however, Nehemiah stood with a clenched fist and said, "Bring it!"

He refused to go flat. He refused to defer his leadership.

Nehemiah is a model of manhood. When confronted with conflict, reject passivity and engage. Refuse to go flat and ignore the issues, hoping they'll disappear. Instead, run at the problem and act without hesitation.

Conflict tempts the best of men to deflate and try to ride out the storm.

Take the Nehemiah approach. Pick up the phone and call. Set that meeting now. Close that deal. Confront that issue. Run at the problems.

Resist the urge to go flat.

THE UNNOTICED CLIMB

Do you not know that in a race all the runners run, but only one gets the prize?
Run in such a way as to get the prize. Everyone who competes in the games goes into strict training.
They do it to get a crown that will not last; but we do it to get a crown that will last forever. 1
Corinthians 9:24-25

The Three Sisters are volcanic peaks in Oregon's Cascade Range. The peaks are cleverly named Faith, Hope, and Charity. Conquering the Sisters in a day requires an eighteen-mile trek and a 9,000 ft. gain in elevation. Climbing the peaks is an extreme stretch of one's mental, physical, and spiritual capabilities.

I hope to do it one day.

However, a deeper question is how do we climb the mountains of faith, hope, and love in this life? What goals can we set in each of these areas? Goals challenge us to climb the mountains that stand between who we are and who he want to be– who God created us to be.

Remember Abraham Lincoln's quote, "Impossibilities vanish when a man and His God confront a mountain." How do you climb an impossible mountain? You do it one goal at a time, one step at a time.

Goals in the areas of faith, hope, and love demand training along with a little blood, sweat, and tears.

Life is more than being alive. Living means training. Training means working. There are no free rides. Males participate, but never run to exhaustion. Men run. They run hard. Men climb one foot at a time, goal by goal, slow and steady until they've conquered the mountains of faith, hope, and love.

The problem is that we take pictures from the summit and not along the journey. The blood, sweat, and tears accompanying the climb often go tragically unnoticed.

Climb anyway. Start training today. Slow and steady. Enjoy the journey!

RUNNING AIMLESSLY

Therefore I do not run like a man running aimlessly; I do not fight like a man beating the air. No, I beat my body and make it my slave so that after I have preached to others, I myself will not be disqualified for the prize.
1 Corinthians 9:26-27

People respond in many ways when confronted with the idea of goal setting. Sometimes I hear spiritual excuses like, "I don't need goals; I just walk by the Spirit and do what God puts on my heart."

Whatever.

Others give more practical excuses: "I'm too busy to set goals." Weak sauce. Or "I'm enjoying life right now. Why would I want to try anything new?" Cop out. I'm of the camp of those who embrace goals as a "God List". As the verse above reveals,

Paul had a definite direction. He knew God's purposes for him. He knew that his "God List" was to take the gospel to the non-Jewish world as the Apostle to the Gentiles (Romans 11:13).

A goal is something not yet accomplished, but is a specific, and measurable objective. A goal is a next-level accomplishment. A dream is transformed into a goal when a man takes measurable action with a specific time deadline.

Reaching a goal takes time, discipline, and (hopefully) God's blessing. But, the first step in goal setting is to make one. Find an objective. Put your dreams to action and write it down.

Goals require discipline. Ingredients to achieve your goal are slow and steady action over a designated time. Reaching a higher level demands discovering new ways to climb.

So pray. Make a goal. Count the cost. Be willing to work toward your new objective. Keep your eyes on the prize.

THE FIRST STEP

Gideon was threshing wheat in a winepress to keep it from the Midianites.
When the angel of the Lord appeared to Gideon, he said, '"The Lord is with you, mighty warrior."
Judges 6:11-12

It took eleven hours to climb Mt. Whitney, the tallest mountain in the contiguous United States. The trek was twenty-two miles round-trip starting at 8,300 feet and ending on the summit at 14,505 feet, with over 6,000 feet of vertical gain. I trained for a year in preparation.

But it was difficult to find a climbing partner. Everyone had excuses. One man actually said I was crazy but climbed Mt. Whitney one year after I did. I finally met Jared, who agreed to be my climbing partner. Jared was willing to take that first step.

Like climbing Mt. Whitney, Gideon's first step as a "mighty warrior" was over the wine press. The first step is the toughest.

When the angel visited Gideon he was threshing wheat in a wine press, likely only two to three feet tall and, at most, six feet in diameter. Can you imagine the effort required to thresh wheat while bent over hiding?

Admittedly, Gideon was the weakest of the weak, the wimpiest of all the wimps, and at the bottom of the food chain. But the angel challenged his perspective. He proclaimed that God was with him and said something really strange to a man hiding in a winepress, "The Lord is with you, mighty warrior."

God sees beyond the hiding places. In the midst of fear, He calls us out of the wine press to embrace our destiny. Gideon will be remembered not because of his family tree but because he had the guts to take the first step over the wall of fear.

What wine press is holding you back today?

NIGHT TERRORS

You will not fear the terror of the night, not the arrow that flies by day.
Psalm 91:5

Hunting California's A-zone is a much different experience than hunting Western Oregon's "rain" zone. Though separated by nearly 1,000 miles, I continue to hunt the same Coast Ridge Range I hunted as a young man in California. But the conditions are vastly different.

In California I'd gear up, like a desert soldier, to endure one-hundred-degree heat and drought-like conditions. Yet, in Oregon, I dress in heavy gear to overcome severe wet weather and often freezing conditions. One thing that doesn't change is the pre-dawn hike to the hunting spot.

The black silence of the pre-dawn is frightening. All my attention is on the headlamp beam and the outlined Lord's Prayer I use as a replacement for the fear that builds with each step. I'm acutely aware that a predator could be lurking just beyond my light beam. To dwell on these thoughts of death is terrifying.

Sometimes all that can be seen are the raindrops pelting my face. In the rain I can't hear a thing. I'm completely vulnerable to attack. In reality, however it's my headlamp that's screaming to all the predators, "A human is coming, a human is coming. He smells dangerous and is formed in the image of God! Run!"

Then I remember and take courage, "The Lord is my light and my salvation—whom shall I fear? The Lord is the stronghold of my life—of whom shall I be afraid?" (Psalm 27:1)

I keep climbing.

Step by step. Slow and steady. Slow and steady.

TEAM MEETING SIX:
BATTLE TO FIGHT

> *"Great men suffer greatly in order to be great. Heroic men must first endure heroic struggles with themselves."*
> ~Steven Mansfield

What did you take away from last week's study and daily readings? What are you still processing? What challenged your current paradigm? What inspired you to grow as a man?

Life is not some downhill coast on your scooter. Life is difficult. It's a legs-pumping climb up a steep mountain. Life is a fight. Life is a battle.

Share one battle you've been fighting. Is there something preventing you from living out the wild side of the life God has for you?

If you aren't fighting to become your best version in Christ, it's because you are not.

In his classic book for men, Wild at Heart, John Eldredge writes that every man has a battle to fight. Generally speaking, what does this mean?

Do not hide your battles in the dark. Expose them to the light. Make them public. Rally others to your battlefield.

Where in Scripture can you find men who fought personal battles?

TEAM MEETING AT A GLANCE

- Opening Prayer, Weekly Announcements
- Personal and Victory Stories
- Each man will share his story—one man per week until all men have shared.
- After all men have shared their personal story, allow time each week for them to share victory stories.
- Weekly Study Closing Prayer
- Closing Prayer

> *"Masculinity is not something given to you, but something you gain. And you gain it by winning small battles with honor."*
> ~Norman Mailer

Listen as the great Apostle Paul struggles with "The Conflict of Two Natures".

"For we know that the Law is spiritual, but I am of flesh, sold into bondage to sin. For what I am doing, I do not understand; for I am not practicing what I would like to do, but I am doing the very thing I hate. But if I do the very thing I do not want to do, I agree with the Law, confessing that the Law is good. So now, no longer am I the one doing it, but sin, which dwells in me.

For I know that nothing good dwells in me, that is, in my flesh; for the willing is present in me, but the doing of the good is not. For the good that I want, I do not do, but I practice the very evil that I do not want. But if I am doing the very thing I do not want, I am no longer the one doing it, but sin which dwells in me.

I find then the principle that evil is present in me, the one who wants to do good. For I joyfully concur with the law of God in the inner man, but I see a different law in the members of my body, waging war against the law of my mind and making me a prisoner of the law of sin which is in my members.

Wretched man that I am! Who will set me free from the body of this death?"
Romans 7:14-24

What truths do we know about sin? How does sin affect us? What collateral damage do we see from sin?
Romans 3:9-10, 3:21-24, 5:6-8, 6:20-23, and Hebrews 4:15

Sin Kills! It kills relationships! It kills destinies! It killed the Son of God!

How are sin and temptation different? Is temptation a sin?
Matthew 4:1-11 and James 1:13-15

What does 1 Corinthians 10:12-13 teach us about temptation?

What guardrails do you have in place? What boundaries do you have to protect those you love from you?
Deuteronomy 22:8, Matthew 7:13-14, Proverbs 16:17, and 27:12

> *"The things we celebrated before Christ we're ashamed of now Shame leads to secrets. Secrets can lead to bondage."*
> ~Anonymous

Remember The Ten Marriage-Saving Nevers from The Trailhead: Protecting Integrity?

#1 Never develop an emotional connection to a person of the opposite sex.

#2 Never be alone with a person of the opposite sex (meals, meetings, mingling) unless at work with open door, window, or somebody close by.

#3 Never engage in any negative talk about your spouse with a person of the opposite sex.

#4 Never compliment a person of the opposite sex unless your spouse is woven into the compliment.

#5 Never have a longstanding counseling/mentoring (more than two meetings) relationship with a person of the opposite sex.

#6 Never make physical contact in a non-casual way (or place) with a person of the opposite sex. Side hugs only please.

#7 Never make rude, course, or sexual comments especially to a person of the opposite sex (or anyone for that matter).

#8 Never give a gift or card that is only from you to a person of the opposite sex. Make all gifts from "us".

#9 Never have non-business-related conversations (includes social media) with a person of the opposite sex.

#10 Never assume your spouse is living by your standards! Stay Engaged.

Where do you need to be fierce in your battle against sin? What hindrances or entangling sins do you need to repent of?
Hebrews 12:1-2

Where has sin softened you? Where has it made you apathetic? What secrets are you hiding?

Break into groups of three or four.

What is the dominant sin in your life?

Take a moment to pray for each other.

STUDY NOTES

<hr />
<hr />
<hr />
<hr />
<hr />
<hr />
<hr />
<hr />
<hr />
<hr />
<hr />
<hr />
<hr />

For the next five days, read the following entries from our **The Field Guide: A Bathroom Book for Men.**

We hope they challenge and encourage you to get in the great Arena for God. See you on the Arena Floor!

PLAYING ARMY

The Lord is my light and my salvation—whom shall I fear? The Lord is the stronghold
of my life—of whom shall I be afraid? When evil men advance against me to devour my flesh, when
my enemies and my foes attack me, they will stumble and fall. Though an army besiege me, my heart
will not fear; though war break out against me, even then will I be confident.
Psalm 27:1-3

A weekend tradition with the neighborhood kids was playing army. The rules were simple. One team would hide in a field while the other hunted them down with their makeshift guns. Pointing your weapon at an unsuspecting target made a kill when followed by, "Bang, you're dead."

I grew up watching the Vietnam War on the evening news. Although intrigued by it, I had a tremendous fear of going to war. Would I be brave enough to fight?

Would I be willing to die for my country? Would I get wounded or maimed? I never had to find out. However, countless numbers of heroes have stood in my place. And I am grateful.

Maybe that is why Psalm 27:1-3 is so meaningful, "When evil men advance against me to devour my flesh, when my enemies and my foes attack me, they will stumble and fall. Though an army besiege me, my heart will not fear; though war break out against me, even then will I be confident."

Fear is not just experiencing the feelings of danger. It's how the danger is handled. Some are frozen by fear. Others run away. But bravery stands to fight when fear shows its ugly face, and everything in a man is begging him to run.

Fear is the means to the end of either courage or cowardice. If, however, "The Lord is the stronghold of my life", I will stand in the midst of it and run to the fray instead of retreating from it.

BLOCKING BABY JESUS

The One who breaks open the way will go up before them;
they will break through the gate and go out.
Micah 2:13

I often wake up with neck pain as a reminder of a sacrifice for my college football brothers. In the traditional "I formation" the fullback's main responsibility was to block for the tailback. In four years of football, I carried the football less than 20 times, but had the privilege of blocking for a great back that led our conference in yards gained.

After graduation I returned to watch him play. After the game he expressed his frustration with gaining only half the yards on twice as many carries, "They just won't block the way you did."

It was an honor to have my sacrifice recognized. You can imagine the impact of two 220-pound men colliding head on at full speed. Multiply that by thirty running plays a game over a season and you have chronic neck pain.

The blocking back, as well as the offensive lineman, sacrifices for his team. Twenty years later my neck agrees.

Men are drawn to the memory of sacrifice. If Jesus played football, my bet is that he would have been a blocking back or offensive lineman. In Romans 3:21 we read, "The righteousness of God has been manifested."

In other words, God has done something great to reveal His power to bring us into a right relationship with Him. This sacrifice is called a "gift of His grace" (Romans 3:24).

Sin blocks our way to God and someone needs to break through on our behalf. Jesus punched a hole in Heaven for us to enter into! That impact was "His blood".

No man can forget this great sacrifice made by Jesus.

Have you?

KEEPING SCORE

This is what the Lord says to the house of Israel: "Seek me and live; do not seek Bethel, do not go to Gilgal, do not journey to Beersheba. For Gilgal will surely go into exile, and Bethel will be reduced to nothing." Seek the Lord and live, or he will sweep through the house of Joseph like a fire; it will devour, and Bethel will have no one to quench it.
Amos 5:4-6

Years ago, I started a summer 3-D archery tournament for the men of my church. 3-D archery is like redneck golf. Archers walk a course shooting dozens of wild game replicas. Scores are based on how close an archer hits to the bulls-eye.

Nearly twenty men paid an entrance fee to shoot together for a competition that could earn them a dozen new arrows worth around one hundred bucks. The person with the best average score after a minimum of five sessions won the tournament.

One man was so frustrated with his shooting that he actually got rid of his bow mid-season and bought a new one. He still placed second. Keep your participation trophy. Men keep score.

Men keep score by the size of their homes, cost of their cars, beauty of their wives, success of their kids, cash in their accounts, and the list goes on. Even the local church values success not by people's hearts, but account ledgers and Sunday attendance. Listen to pastors interact if you're not convinced.

A great temptation is to be a mile wide and an inch deep. When our eyes are so focused on conquering the finite things of life, we're tempted to neglect the God who gave it. Go ahead, keep score, but make sure you're playing the right game.

We're wired to be "more than conquerors" (Romans 8:37) which only comes through radical commitment to Jesus. A man's trophies will fade, but how he seeks his God will last an eternity.

Shoot your arrows straight. Shoot them at the God who made you.

LEVEL GROUND

Sow for yourselves righteousness, reap the fruit of unfailing love, and break up your unplowed ground; for it is time to seek the Lord, until he comes and showers righteousness on you.
Hosea 10:12

One backpacking challenge is to find a camp close to cover, water, and on level ground. On one trip we located a grove barely large enough to fit our bivouac tents. But the area sloped requiring us to level the surrounding area by kicking away the high ground. We then kicked away enough dirt, enabling our tents to rest on level ground.

Relationships aren't much different. They require a little leveling— kicking away dirt —to find level ground. Part of the pursuit of God is to make sure our horizontal relationships are on the level, so to speak.

When our horizontal relationships are on level ground, we're positioned to make our vertical relationship healthy as well. If, however, any of our earthly relationships aren't on level ground, neither will be our relationship with God. They too work hand-in-hand (Matthew 18:15-17).

The discipline needed to pursue healthy relationships is like breaking sloped ground. It requires our constant kicking. Sometimes that kicking is in someone's backside!

Where is your life not on level ground and putting you in danger of rolling off the mountain? Are there relationships in your life that are sloping the wrong way or beginning to slide? Maybe, they're on shaky ground?

Start kicking.

Level the horizontal playing field so you can experience the fullness of your vertical relationship.

WITH

Look to the Lord and his strength; seek his face always.
Psalm 105:4

After a broken arm ended his eighth-grade football season, we decided to beef up my son James in preparation for freshman football. He was small for his age, so we designed a strength program and jumped right in.

I smiled at James' awkward movements. His muscles struggled to balance the heavy weights. After a week or so, he caught on and the rest is history. James went on to play college football.

We all start somewhere. James grew strong by working out with someone stronger. There is depth to the truth in this statement. Strength breeds strength.

We're only as strong as those we choose to associate with. Birds of a feather flock together. Like begets like. You are becoming like those you spend the most time with.

Lock arms with men older, wiser, and spiritually stronger than you. Guess what – you'll become like them. Associate with those weaker and you will become the same.

Physical strength fades away. Human strength fails. It's a vapor. Men, even the strongest, are just men. The only strength needed for life is found in the Source of all strength.

Maybe that's why an aging Paul wrote, "Therefore we do not lose heart. Though outwardly we are wasting away, yet inwardly we are being renewed day by day" (2 Corinthians 4:16).

Seek the Strength that never fades. Seek the Strong One and let His power make you the man you were designed to be. "Not by might nor by power, but by My Spirit,' says the Lord of hosts" (Zechariah 4:6).

Refuse to work for God. Instead, work with Him.

TEAM MEETING SEVEN:
OF GUTS AND

> *"All daring and courage, all iron endurance of misfortune make for a finer and nobler type of manhood."*
> ~Theodore Roosevelt, 1897

What did you take away from last week's study and daily readings? What are you still processing? What challenged your current paradigm? What inspired you to grow as a man?

Today's study is dedicated to my high school football coach Jim Fazio. Coach Fazio was a short, fiery Italian with a quirky way of getting his point across. His athletes loved him, but you never knew how he might react. We were playing Cabrillo High School under Friday night lights during my junior year of high school and Coach was struggling for the right call from the sidelines.

In the heat of battle I made a mistake I'll never forget. I yelled (there may or may not have been hand gestures involved), "Hurry up!"

He got a scary look in his eyes, called time out, and waved me over with his index finger. He got on the tips of his toes, grabbed my facemask, and pulled me to eye level.

I'll never forget the words he spoke as Dad, an assistant coach, watched nearby, "I don't care who you are. If you ever do that again I'll personally kick your &^*&# @%$!" I walked back to the huddle and realized he never gave me the defensive call!

Coach Fazio regularly warned, "Don't get upset when I yell and scream at you. It means I still believe in you. But the day I stop coaching, and yelling, you'd better get nervous because that's the day you'll be benched."

When was the last time you were called out? What happened? How did you respond?

76

TEAM MEETING AT A GLANCE

- Opening Prayer, Weekly Announcements
- Personal and Victory Stories
- Each man will share his story — one man per week until all men have shared.
- After all men have shared their personal story, allow time each week for them to share victory stories.
- Weekly Study Closing Prayer
- Closing Prayer

> *"A friend is busy watching our back, while an enemy is often kissing our butt."*
> ~Anonymous

Friendships are defined by how open and willing they are to call each other out.

Discuss the anonymous quote, "True friends have the courage to call us out."

How we handle being confronted says a lot about our humility, depth, willingness to grow, as well as the strength of our relationships.

Someone read Proverbs 27:5-6 out loud.

Better is open rebuke than hidden love.
Wounds from a friend can be trusted, but an enemy multiplies kisses.

What does verse 5 mean? What is an "open rebuke"? What is "hidden love"?
Proverbs 28:23

Sometimes a friend needs to be called out, some sooner than later. Sometimes I am that friend!

What are some reasons you choose to stay on the sidelines rather than confront? What does our unwillingness to confront say about us? About our friend?

What is the best way to handle things when someone rightfully, lovingly calls you over to the sidelines, grabs your facemask, and calls you out?
Proverbs 25:12, Galatians 6:1-2, and Ephesians 4:14-1

How you handle being called over to the sidelines is a defining moment.

What is the goal when rebuking, calling out, a brother? Why would you call out someone you care about?
Proverbs 1:22-25, 30, 3:11-12, 13:1, 17:10, and 19:25

> *"Better is open rebuke than hidden love.*
> *Wounds from a friend can be trusted, but an enemy multiplies kisses."*
> Proverbs 27:5-6

My best friend calls out the best in me. What process should be employed when calling someone out?
Proverbs 9:8, Matthew 18:15-18, and Titus 3:9-11

What are some solid guidelines when rebuking a brother?
Mark 8:33, Luke 17:3-4, and Ephesians 4:15

If we say we have someone's back maybe we should let them know when the knife's coming.

Let's pull the facemask to eye level. What is meant in Proverbs 27:6a, "Wounds from a friend can be trusted"?
Proverbs 24:26

What about, "but an enemy multiplies kisses" (Proverbs 27:6b)? How is flattery damaging to a relationship? Should you question the depth of any relationship that never pushes back?
Matthew 26:48-49

What is one danger when we don't have the guts to call time out, and call a friend to the sidelines to speak the hard truth in love? What does our unwillingness to call out someone we care about say about us?

Break into groups of three or four.

Who do you need to call over to the sidelines?

Take a moment to pray for each other.

STUDY NOTES

_____

_____

_____

_____

_____

_____

_____

_____

_____

_____

_____

_____

_____

For the next five days, read the following entries from our **The Field Guide: A Bathroom Book for Men.**

We hope they challenge and encourage you to get in the great Arena for God. See you on the Arena Floor!

DUCKS IN A ROW

But Jehoshaphat also said to the king of Israel,
"First seek the counsel of the Lord."
1 Kings 22:5

When duck hunting, I set my decoys in a V-formation from the blind outward. I typically arrange the decoys by species with mallards in close, then teal and widgeons, with the pintails furthest out. The secret, obviously, is to imitate live ducks on the water.

I group the decoys by species because of a truth I've learned. Birds of a feather flock together. Like begets like. Water seeks its own level. Men are a lot like ducks.

We seek out like-minded people for our social circles. We want the advice of men who (we hope) will tell us what we need to hear, even if it's not what we want to hear.

Jehoshaphat and Ahab, on the surface, appear to be seekers of truth. But all Ahab really wanted was affirmation and not the truth. Ahab knew his 400 prophets were not speaking the truth, but when confronted with the truth (1 Kings 22:4-23) he chose to ignore it. Instead, finding other men to affirm his plan, went against God's truth, and ultimately died for it.

We're not too far from Ahab.

We're really good at working for God, but not so good at working with Him. We bring our preconceived agendas to the field and seek affirmation instead of the truth. If we really want to get our ducks in a row we should seek God's truth.

Then, rally men who have the guts to sharpen us based on that truth. But be willing to accept the truth from God no matter how hard it may be.

Part of manhood is being obedient to God's truth even if it hurts. It's seeking counsel from men who'll tell us what we need - not what we may want.

WEAKNESS

But he said to me, "My grace is sufficient for you, for my power is made perfect in weakness."
2 Corinthians 12:9

Six o'clock came early after the two-day drive, on only three hours of sleep, hauling more than one hundred high school students and staff to Hume Lake Christian Camps. Should I sleep in until eight or do my annual prayer walk around the lake?

Ultimately, tradition won out, and I was up and praying for God to strengthen my sleep deprived body as the beams of light crested the Sierra Nevada Mountains.

I'm so thankful to see God's brilliance through creation. I've been a part of many discussions surrounding the Apostle Paul's "thorn in the flesh" mentioned in 2 Corinthians 12:7-10. Let me share my thoughts about this.

Paul never fully recovered from losing his eyesight when saved on the road to Damascus in Acts 9:1-18. But he couldn't go to the local optometrist to have laser surgery. He couldn't renew his contact lens prescription. He couldn't put on his reading glasses (for us older guys).

A loss of eyesight would have dramatically hindered Paul's ministry. It would have been a "thorn." We know Paul had some serious vision issues from a clue in Galatians 6:11, "See what large letters I use as I write to you with my own hand!"

We also know he begged God for healing and God replied, "My grace is sufficient for you, for my power is made perfect in weakness." God allowed Paul's poor eyesight (I believe) so He could use him in a greater measure.

I don't want to judge the intent of God, but we know one reason for this thorn was to prevent him from becoming "conceited" (2 Corinthians 12:7).

Thank God for your weaknesses. They are a gift to see that His grace really is sufficient for you.

WINE PRESS

Go in the strength you have and save Israel out of Midian's hand. Am I not sending you?
Judges 6:14

I love Gideon's story. He's the classic underdog. Check it out. In Judges, God approaches Gideon in a wine press, threshing wheat, while hiding from the Midianite army. An ancient wine press was six to ten feet in diameter and only two or three feet high.

Threshing wheat was an aggressive movement. Imagine a grown man, bent over on his knees, beating the wheat to a pulp, terrified and scanning the horizon for invaders.

How humiliating for a grown man!

Gideon's half-tribe of Manasseh (Genesis 48:1-14) was the smallest of the tribes of Israel. Gideon's family was the weakest in his tribe. Gideon was the weakest in his family. Gideon was the least of the least, the weakest of the weak, and the wimpiest of the wimps. But the angel of the Lord saw something in Gideon; "The Lord is with you, mighty warrior" (Judges 6:12).

God uses us where we are, not where we think we should be. God will change you, as you trust in Him. God transformed Gideon into a mighty warrior. Joshua, Moses' administrative assistant (Deuteronomy 1:38), was chosen to lead the nation into the elusive land of promise.

"Today I will begin to exalt you in the eyes of all Israel, so they may know that I am with you as I was with Moses" (Joshua 3:7).

God changed Joshua too. Gideon was just a man—a weak one. And God chose to use him. But Gideon had to stand up, get out of the wine press, and step forward by faith.

What wine press is keeping you down today? Step out of the bondage of fear and allow God to change you into one of His mighty warriors.

CAPTURE THE FORT

It is God who arms me with strength and makes my way perfect...
You armed me with strength for battle; you made my adversaries bow at my feet.
2 Samuel 22:33 and 40

For a year I prepared an impeccable plan of victory for Hume Lake's Capture
the Fort paintball game. The fort is made out of old tires, stands four feet tall, about twelve feet long,
and four feet wide with a small opening in the east wall.

Defending teams have high ground and must ward off attackers while opposing teams attempt to
safely place a teammate inside before being shot.

My victory plan was to form a human phalanx and charge the fort. The larger players, like me, led the
way acting as human shields for the smaller players. Hiding the smaller targets enabled us to sneak
someone inside the fort unscathed. Being the tip of the spear

I received eighteen hits during our offensive. Several of those were from overindulgent young men in
my youth group.

We won. It was worth every welt.

When I think of a strong fortress, I'm reminded of that tire fort at Hume.
In David's song of deliverance God is called a "strong fortress" (Psalm 31:2).

- I think of Jesus taking my hits (Isaiah 53:5).
- I think of God paving the way for my success.
- I think of a protector who guards my heart (Philippians 4:7).
- I think of a Savior whose work on the cross is impenetrable to enemy
attacks (Ephesians 6:16).
- I think of a Father who protects all who have chosen His fort (Acts 4:12
and John 1:12).

BE SOMETHING

Be strong and courageous, because you will lead these people to inherit the land I swore to their forefathers to give them. Be strong and very courageous. Be careful to obey all the law my servant Moses gave you; do not turn from it to the right or to the left, that you may be successful wherever you go... Have I not commanded you? Be strong and courageous.
Joshua 1:6-7, 9

After a quarter of a century of sitting second chair behind senior leaders I've learned that working in a support role has its unique challenges. One of them is that the second chair employee learns to depend on those sitting above to protect them.

You learn to trust your leader in the second chair. But life in the first chair is much different. We see that in today's passage where three times in three verses God commands Joshua to "be strong and (very) courageous."

Moses is dead. Now Joshua's the leader. He's the one calling the shots. He's sitting in the first chair. He's the one taking the hits. He needs the strength, and most of all, courage. To "be strong" is a choice to act, move, and do something.

I've never met a man who was content to be nothing. God has wired men for significance—to "be" something to someone. Strength, however, is a decisive action.

Weakness is not the opposite of strength. The opposite of strength is passivity. The passive man is soft, lacking spiritual punch. The passive life lacks the ability to move. Adam was weak because he chose the path of passivity rather than protecting his woman. Paul was strong from constantly kicking in doors (1 Corinthians 16:9).

Rejecting passivity is a choice. It's a choice to "be" something for someone. Don't let life happen. Trust God to make it happen. The easiest road for Joshua would've been to nominate Caleb as the next leader (Deuteronomy 1:38).

But he didn't. Instead, he chose to "be" something for someone.

TEAM MEETING EIGHT:
WHO HAS YOUR BACK?

> *"How you handle the secrets of your friends will either be a fragrant aroma or a rancid stench."*
> ~Jim Ramos

What did you take away from last week's study and daily readings? What are you still processing? What challenged your current paradigm? What inspired you to grow as a man?

Think hard on this one. Let's go around the room and answer the question, "Who's got my back?" Who can you depend on? In a dark alley, who do you want with you? Who can you call at 2:00 AM?

Today's meeting title was inspired by rock band Creed's song, Who's Got my Back? The end of the chorus asks, "So what is the truth now?"

Discuss the relationship between truth and those who have your back.

It's not the hard truth that ultimately wounds us, but the cold silence of gutless cowards we call friends.

How do you deal with the tension of speaking truth to those who are pursuing God (Christian brothers) versus those who aren't?

TEAM MEETING AT A GLANCE

- Opening Prayer, Weekly Announcements
- Personal and Victory Stories
- Each man will share his story — one man per week until all men have shared.
- After all men have shared their personal story, allow time each week for them to share victory stories.
- Weekly Study Closing Prayer
- Closing Prayer

> *"Kin-blood is not spoilt by water."*
> ~Heinrich der Glîchezære (1180)

Someone please read Proverbs 27:9-10 out loud.

Perfume and incense bring joy to the heart,
and the pleasantness of one's friend springs from his earnest
counsel. Do not forsake your friend and the friend of your father,
and do not go to your brother's house when disaster strikes you
—better a neighbor nearby than a brother far away."

How are "perfume and incense" compared to the "earnest counsel" of a friend? Why would these two be compared to each other?

Which of these translations of Proverbs 27:9b do you prefer and why?

"The sweetness of one's friend is the fruit of hearty counsel."
~Darby Translation

"So a man's counsel is sweet to his friend."
~New American Standard

"The sweetness of a friend comes from his earnest counsel."
~English Standard Version

"The sweetness of his friend from the counsel of soul."
~Hebrew translation

"The counsel of a friend is sweeter than one's own advice."
~G.R. Driver translation

"A friend who is available is better than a relative who is not."
~Expositor's Bible Commentary (Pg. 1097)

How should a friend watch your back? What does this mean to you? What does having someone's back look like?
Job 16:20-21, Ecclesiastes 4:10, and Proverbs 17:17

> *"Blood is thicker than water."*
> John Ray 1670

Let's tackle verse 10. Compare Proverbs 27:10, "Better a neighbor nearby than a brother far away" with Proverbs 18:24, "One who has unreliable friends soon comes to ruin, but there is a friend who sticks closer than a brother." What are your thoughts?

Relationships see the context of our situations. Proximity sees more clearly than the long-distance relationship.

How do you understand verse 10:
"Do not go to your brother's house when disaster strikes you—better a neighbor nearby than a brother far away"?

Which of these statements is true? "Better a neighbor nearby than a brother far away" or "Blood is thicker than water?"

Finish the sentence: I'm the kind of friend that _____

Here's a funny story about a friend who did not have his friend's back:
Two adventurous teenage boys were out exploring when they came upon a set of large bear tracks. They decided to follow the tracks, moving with extreme caution. Suddenly, from behind a rock, jumped a giant Grizzly bear.

Standing squarely in front of them, the bear beat on his chest and roared, it's terrible sounds echoing off the canyon walls.

Horrified, the two boys turned to run for their lives. Just then, one of the boys dropped to the floor and started untying his heavy hiking boots. He whipped the boots off, jammed on his running shoes, and began tying the laces.

His friend yelled, "Come on, man! Let's get out of here! Why in the world are you changing shoes? We don't have much of a chance of outrunning that bear anyway!" Lunging to his feet, the first boy replied, "I don't have to outrun that bear. All I have to do is outrun you!"

Men have a tendency to isolate themselves from got-your-back relationships with other men. This is not only unwise, it's dangerous. Why do you need at least one man like this in your life?

Break into groups of three or four.

Whose back do you have? Why? Would they agree? Who's got your back?

Pray for those people.

Take a moment today and pray for each other.

> *"Keep your friends close and your enemies closer."*
> ~Secular Proverb

STUDY NOTES

_____

_____

_____

_____

_____

_____

_____

_____

_____

_____

_____

_____

For the next five days, read the following entries from our **The Field Guide: A Bathroom Book for Men.**

We hope they challenge and encourage you to get in the great Arena for God. See you on the Arena Floor!

HIGH GROUND

Do not grieve, for the joy of the LORD is your strength.
It is God who arms me with strength and keeps my way secure... You armed me with strength for
battle; you humbled my adversaries before me.
Psalm 18: 32 and 39

We stopped at the little Chevron station in Prairie City, Oregon on our way to scout our hunting spot in the Strawberry Wilderness. There's a law in Oregon that makes it illegal to pump your own gas, so when the weathered gas attendant introduced himself as Kelly, I asked about the basin we were scouting.

He grinned, "If you're in good enough shape to reach that basin, you'll see big bucks. Big bucks live up high."

We learned the hard way that getting to high ground requires big risks and big-time effort. In today's passage, twice we read that God "arms me with strength." Not only does God arm us with strength, but gives us the strength needed on the climb to higher ground.

"He makes my feet like the feet of a deer; he enables me to stand on the heights" (Psalm 18:33).

God feeds us in the valley but strengthens us on the climb to higher ground. To have "the feet of a deer (18:33)," "hands trained for battle (18:34)," and "arms that can bend a bronze bow (18:34)" isn't for everyone. It's reserved for those courageous souls willing to pay the sweat equity needed to summit the mountain of God.

The line between passion and stupidity can be thin to those on the outside looking in. But too many men are comfortable being fat in the valley and won't get fit for their climb to high ground.

Males simply aren't willing to make the sacrifices necessary to summit.

It's a man's job. Only a man can make the climb. Males need not apply.

MESSY PEOPLE

Where there are no oxen, the manger is empty,
but from the strength of an ox comes an abundant harvest.
Proverbs 14:4

I once took a young man on his first backpacking adventure. All he had for rain gear were noisy snowboarding pants and a jacket. He literally squeaked when he walked! I probably made more noise than him by constantly telling him to be quiet.

Squeak. Squeak. Squeak.

As the hunt progressed, the rain relented. He not only spotted the buck we ended up shooting, but helped process and carry it four miles back to the truck. It was an amazing time with him, in spite of his squeaky snowboarding pants.

My memorable time with him reminded me of a book I read several years earlier called Messy Spirituality by the late Mike Yaconelli. In his book, Yaconelli speaks in depth that faith is much sloppier than meets the eye.

Men often put up a tough-guy veneer, but underneath life is a mess.

Men are stubborn, resistant, and often difficult to reach. Our culture has emasculated men until all we hear is the squeak, but don't know how to stop it. But even that guy is worth reaching.

When you reach a man, you reach his family. Men are a leader's greatest asset and worth the time and effort to pursue. Men are worth the noise they make. Men will make ministry a little messy, but the potential added to your life and ministry is worth the mess.

Remember, when a man gets it, everyone wins. He is like the ox that, through him, becomes "an abundant harvest."

Squeak. Squeak. Squeak.

KEEPING COURAGE UP

I urge you to keep up your courage…So keep up your courage, men, for I have faith in God that it will happen just as he told me.
Acts 27:22 and 25

On my first trip to Maui I went snorkeling and, to my amazement, I could float in the salt water with the best of them. Remove the snorkel and mask, put me in fresh water, and I epitomize Bob Seger's song, Like a Rock.

I can swim, but it takes so much work to stay afloat, my body tires easily, and I begin to sink. I'm glad no one can see how much I must be sweating underwater.

Courage is like me trying to swim. It takes a lot of work. Without work, the propensity of my body is to sink. Courage operates the same way.

It's work. It's a choice. It takes effort to keep courage up.

Fight to, "Keep up your courage." In Acts 27, Paul's ship is sinking and twice, in four verses, he admonishes the crewman to, "Keep up your courage."

When fear begins to pull a man under, he must fight to keep courage afloat. Courage takes work to keep buoyant. It takes movement. Courage is not static. A man may swim through the currents of life one day and drown in the undertow of apathy the next.

Courage is a fight. Courage is a verb. Courage must be kept up.

When life's undertow begins to wear you down, tread water. Move your arms. Identify the resistances in your life and begin swimming. It's there that you'll begin to keep your courage up.

TREADING WATER

Be on your guard; stand firm in the faith; be men of courage; be strong. Do everything in love.
1 Corinthians 16:13-14

The first time I heard a man call other men boys was at Family Life's "Weekend to Remember" couple's retreat. The speaker slapped my idea of manhood in the face. For the first time I realized I was, in many ways, a boy. At the time I was forty.

I'm often selfish, fail to accept responsibility, and choose pleasure over sacrifice. I know a lot of forty-year-old boys beside myself. I'm sure you do too. Age does not make the man. It takes something more.

Males will often oscillate between a man and a boy. Boys act like selfish, spoiled children—self-serving. Boys are parents, but not fathers, spouses but not husbands, acquaintances but not friends, and Christians but not disciples. Anatomy doesn't make you a man. Actions do.

Being a man takes courage. God calls men to be courageous leaders in the home, guarding against the enemy's attacks. I wholeheartedly support strong women. But I'm absolutely pro-man. Men are the problem and the solution. Where are the magnum men in the Church?

Where is their leadership?

They speak courageous words, but live cowardly lives. They talk about leading the family while lounging on the furniture. God gave men the awesome privilege of leading the family and being a priest in his home.

It's time for males to grow up. It's time for men to step up. It's time to repent of our boyish ways and grow up.

"When I became a man, I put the ways of childhood behind me."
1 Corinthians 13:11

EARNEST EXPECTATIONS

I eagerly expect and hope that I will in no way be ashamed, but will have sufficient courage so that now as always Christ will be exalted in my body, whether by life or by death.
Philippians 1:20

We were up to our chests in mud, pushing an empty duck boat to the ramp. A group of bird watchers, and assumed anti-hunters (based on their laughter), watched the three of us struggle through the muck and shame in another one of Morro Bay's infamous minus tides. And we never even shot a duck.

Three 230-plus-pound men pushing a boat through the mud was quite a sight!
Our story reminds me of the Apostle Paul who had an "earnest expectation and hope" (NASB) that God would deliver him. Paul knew beyond the shadow of a doubt that

God would pull him through life's muddy struggles. So often men try to pull themselves through the mud. We're self-made, rugged men, right? We believe in Jesus, but trust in ourselves. We seek Christ, but place our hope in our own strength (Zechariah 4:6).

Eventually, however, we grow weary. We get worn out and we realize we've been pulling the wrong boat. The once white-hot fire for God is replaced with the lukewarm pursuits of the world (Mark 4:18-19). The once bold flame of courage becomes a flickering ember of cowardice.

When life is nothing more than pursuing wealth, it's easy to settle into a comfortable existence. But the comfortable life lacks courage. It takes little or no courage to be comfortable.

Courage is found when a man steps out of the world he knows into the unknown adventure that God has to offer.

If you want to walk on water, you need to get out of the boat.

Get into your discomfort zone and find life again.

TEAM MEETING NINE:
SHARPENING YOUR FACE

> *"One man in a thousand, Solomon says, will stick closer than a brother. And it's worthwhile seeking him half your days if you find him before the other. Nine-hundred and ninety-nine depend on what the world sees in you, but the Thousandth Man will stand your friend with the whole round world against you."*
> ~ Rudyard Kipling
> *The Thousandth Man (poem)*

What did you take away from last week's study and daily readings? What are you still processing? What challenged your current paradigm? What inspired you to grow as a man?

Thinking back over the lyrics to the band Survivor's classic "Rocky" fight song, Eye of the Tiger, I noticed the emboldened words "we" and "us". We do that! Having the eye of the tiger is not something done in isolation. Why is partnership important to "hanging tough, staying hungry" in life?

Relationships affect your face. Think about how your various relationships affect your face, or countenance, such as relationships with your spouse, best friend, son or daughter, boss, coach, fellow employee, and those we call friends?

They make us better or worse than we are, sharper or duller than we are, smarter or dumber than we are, more stable or insecure than we are, stronger or weaker than we are, more of a finisher or quitter than we are, and closer to Jesus or further away.

TEAM MEETING AT A GLANCE

- Opening Prayer, Weekly Announcements
- Personal and Victory Stories
- Each man will share his story—one man per week until all men have shared.
- After all men have shared their personal story, allow time each week for them to share victory stories.
- Weekly Study Closing Prayer
- Closing Prayer

Turn in your Bibles to a classic passage for men found in Proverbs 27:17. Or just read the various translations we've provided for you.

"As iron sharpens iron, so one person sharpens another." (NIV)

"Iron sharpeneth iron; so a man sharpeneth the countenance of his friend." (KJV)

"As iron sharpens iron, so a man sharpens the countenance of his friend." (NKJV)

"As iron sharpens iron, so one man sharpens another." (NASB)

"Iron sharpens iron, and one man sharpens another." (ESV)

When you think of iron sharpening iron, what do you think of? What images come to mind? Have you ever sharpened a knife? What happens? How do you do it?

"The word 'countenance' used in the King James Version above is the Hebrew word pene. Pene is the Hebrew word for face. The word pene (face) must mean here the personality or character of the individual."
~Expositors Bible commentary

Wow, that's cool! Now you understand why Eye of the Tiger introduced today's study. How could you translate Proverbs 27:17 based on what you now know about the Hebrew word pene (face)? Come up with some creative translations of your own.

Do you still have the eye of the tiger? Or, has life somehow stolen it from you. If you've lost it, take it back!

We're studying ways of sharpening your face, but let's consider dulling relationships. Are there any relationships that have a dulling effect on your faith? Life? Relationships?

> *"Fathers are to sons what blacksmiths are to swords. It is the job of the blacksmith not only to make the sword but also to maintain its edge of sharpness. It is the job of the father to keep his son sharp and save him from the dullness of foolishness. He gives his son that sharp edge through discipline."*
> ~Steve Farrar

Numbers 6:24-27 is another time pene is used for "countenance". How does your Bible translation interpret pene in this passage? What does a sharp face look like? How does it live?

> *"As hard iron, or steel, will bring a knife to a better edge when it is properly whetted against it: so one friend may be the means of exciting another to reflect, (or) dive deeply into, an illustrate subject, without which whetting or excitement, this had never taken place."*
> ~Adam Clarke Commentary

Let's sharpen Ecclesiastes 10:10 with Proverbs 27:17. What do you see? How do these passages work together in friendships? How do they maintain the eye of the tiger?

"Two minds acting on each other become more acute."
~Barnes Notes

Take a moment to compare the characteristics of a sharpening agent (steel or stone) with a sharpening relationship in your life. How is the man of Proverbs 27:17 similar to the subject of Hebrews 4:12-13?

What men have you invited to judge the "thoughts and intentions of your heart"?

> *"But let me sharpen others as the hone gives edge to razors, though itself have none."*
> ~St. Francis of Assisi

Harvard University's Grant Study
A longitudinal study tracking the lives of 268 physically and mentally healthy white, American, male college sophomores at Harvard University (twenty years old) from the classes of 1939–1944 (born in 1919-24). The men continue to be studied to this day. George Vaillant was the study director.

The men were evaluated at least every two years by questionnaires, information from their physicians, and in many cases by personal interviews. Information was gathered about their mental and physical health, career enjoyment, retirement experience and marital quality.

The goal of the study was to identify predictors of healthy aging. Vaillant writes, "It was the capacity for intimate relationships that predicted the flourishing aspects of these men's lives."

In a New York Times article David Brooks argued that close relationships especially in childhood made a "massive difference" in the lives of these men. Of the thirty-one men in the study who were incapable of forming intimate relationships only four are still alive. Of those better at forming relationships over a third are still alive.

How can you be a better face sharpener? Who can you invite to sharpen your face? Have you ever isolated yourself from life-giving, face sharpening relationships?

Break into groups of three or four.

Who is sharpening your face?

Let's pray for the men who sharpen our faces!

Take a moment today and pray for each other.

STUDY NOTES

_____

_____

_____

_____

_____

_____

_____

_____

_____

_____

_____

_____

For the next five days, read the following entries from our **The Field Guide: A Bathroom Book for Men.**

We hope they challenge and encourage you to get in the great Arena for God. See you on the Arena Floor!

DO WORK

David also said to Solomon his son, "Be strong and courageous, and do the work.
Do not be afraid or discouraged, for the Lord God, my God, is with you. He will not fail you or
forsake you until all the work for the service of the temple of the Lord is finished."
1 Chronicles 28:20-21

After a hard day of training, my son James strutted into the living room, pounded his chest, and proclaimed, "I did work in the weight room today." "Did work?" I wondered. I hadn't heard that phrase before. James was talking about something many of us know—being in the weight room doesn't mean the work was done. Being on the team doesn't mean you're in the game. Being a male doesn't mean you're a man.

Courage takes work. Courage isn't sitting on the couch playing video games. It isn't the pastor hiding in the church office telling the church to evangelize. It isn't going with the flow. Courage is a coarse piece of sandpaper rubbing against the grain. Courage without action isn't courage. It presses on without excuse.

It does work.

All experience fear, but fear isn't cowardice until it fails to act. Fear justifies its immobility. Even the most frightened men become heroes when they move forward. Courage does work. Fear does nothing —or the wrong thing.

Action and courage are two sides of the same coin. Courage shouts, *"How long will you lie there, you sluggard? When will you get up from your sleep? A little sleep, a little slumber, a little folding of the hands to rest"*
Proverbs 6:9-10

David also said to Solomon his son, "Be strong and courageous, and do the work.

"Do not be afraid or discouraged, for the Lord God, my God, is with you. He will not fail you or forsake you until all the work for the service of the temple of the Lord is finished."
1 Chronicles 28:20-21

PARTICIPATION TROPHIES

Let love and faithfulness never leave you; bind them around your neck, write them on the tablet of your heart. Then you will win favor and a good name in the sight of God and man.
Proverbs 3:3-4

One disturbing thing about recreational sports is the Participation Trophy. Children receive a medal or trophy at the conclusion of a sport just for participating? Parents pay the price but children get the trophy?

They're meaningless awards that teach children that participation means entitlement. The value of effort and achievement is removed when competition is dumbed down to participation. If you want to put a trophy on your wall, then buy one. Stop trying to reduce victory to participation.

God has wired us to win not just participate. Win, not only on the spiritual battleground, but to "win favor in the sight of God and man" (NASB).

As a man matures in Christ, competition changes from others-focused to God-focused. The adult life is spent competing against one's limits, fears, flesh, and temptations. This is not done to receive a medal or trophy but, according to verse 3, to "let love and faithfulness never leave you." Love and faithfulness are the medals to chase.

The greatest enemy of man isn't Satan. The greatest adversary is the man in the mirror.

"When tempted, no one should say, 'God is tempting me.' For God cannot be tempted by evil, nor does he tempt anyone; but each one is tempted when, by his own evil desire, he is dragged away and enticed" (James 1:13-14).

The godly man's ultimate win is the status of knowing that he has finally defeated selfishness with love and faithfulness.

"Then you will win the favor of a good name in the sight of God and man."
Proverbs 3:4

CHANGING TIRES

Then Abraham spoke up again: "Now that I have been so bold as to speak to the Lord, though I am nothing but dust and ashes, what if the number of the righteous is five less than fifty? Will you destroy the whole city for lack of five people?" "If I find forty-five there," he said, "I will not destroy it."
Genesis 18:27-28

I witnessed a husband drive away from his wife while she was changing a flat tire. Shocked, I approached her to help and she snapped, "I can handle it! I don't need a man to help me!"

I smiled, told her I was going to help her anyway because I'd want a man to help my wife in a similar situation. I fixed her tire while she begrudgingly observed. She thanked me with angry eyes and drove away.

Boldness, like manhood, has been neutered by culture that frowns on chivalrous, bold men. Refuse to throw in the towel of surrender to a castrated form of Christianity. I can only imagine what it must be like for this woman's husband to drive away instead of helping her, in spite of her angry eyes.

Can you imagine the guts Abraham had to have to negotiate with God for the cities of Sodom and Gomorrah? I thought I was bold with the grumpy tire lady. Wow. Abraham's boldness is rare today.

We need more men like him.

Men of this generation, like Abraham, need to be proud of their God-ordained role. It's tempting to walk away from the angry eyes that desperately need our help. Don't be passive to hurting people who need your help but don't know how to receive it. Show up anyway. Walk through the doors. Pick up the tire wrench.

Smile, roll up your sleeves, and refuse to be neutered by those who tragically claim you are not needed. Let the world feel the weight of who you are as a man and let them deal with it.

JELLYBEANS

The wicked put up a bold front, but the upright give thought to his ways.
Proverbs 21:29

Every team I've coached has heard my speech about marshmallows, rocks, and jellybeans. Marshmallows are easy to see. They don't pretend to be something they're not. They're weak and soft and easy to identify.

Rocks are also easy to identify. They bring their history of toughness with them. Their walk matches their talk. Others will testify of their toughness. They're solid, strong, resolute.

Jellybeans, however, are difficult to determine. They talk a big talk. They look hard on the outside, but when push comes to shove, and the going gets tough, they fold. They're soft on the inside even though they might fool you with their hard exterior.

They "put up a bold front" but have nothing to back it up. Maturity and experience teach that bigger doesn't mean better. Louder doesn't mean smarter. Stronger doesn't mean courageous, and vulgar language doesn't mean tougher.

The opposite is usually true. The bold front is a mask hiding the soft insides of the jellybean.

But Proverbs 29:21 says, "the upright give thought to his ways."

A man is more than the front he projects. Manhood is much more than some old school, immature, bold front that couldn't be farther from true masculinity. A man is as a man does.

The target for manhood comes from clues in Scripture. The Men in the Arena's definition of manhood puts the pieces together: "Protecting integrity, fighting apathy, pursuing God passionately, leading courageously, and finishing strong."

LION BOLD

The wicked man flees though no one pursues, but the righteous are as bold as a lion.
Proverbs 28:1

My friend Jim is one of Men in the Arena's "Original 15"— men that were in a Bible Study I started when I was praying about leaving my secure job at a local church to birth an idea God conceived in my heart, which is now Men in the Arena. He played four years in the NFL and is one of the toughest men I know. As I write this, Jim is in his mid-sixties.

Jim loves to tell a story about when he was a teenager and he and two friends went hunting on the Oregon coast. His buddies had guns and all Jim carried was a fixed-blade knife. Somehow, they came between a sow and her cubs, sending momma bear into high alert.

The protective sow charged at the teens. Fearing for their lives they unloaded their guns, missing every shot, and took off running in the opposite direction. Jim, on the other hand, unsheathed his knife and ran at the charging bear screaming all the way. True story. By some miracle the sow decided she'd better protect herself from this wild teenager and retreated. I told you he was tough.

Psychologists tell us that when faced with danger our brain elicits a fight or flight response. Some will run and fight while others will run away. What causes some to be as timid as a mouse and others as "bold as a lion"?

One reason I believe "the wicked man flees" is because his life begins and ends with himself. He has no great cause transcending his life. With nothing but today to live for, he runs to run another day. Not so with a man of God. He charges when others retreat, recognizing this might be the defining moment he was created for.

So instead of running away, he runs at troubles, either to the hill he will die on or the moment that will define him.

TEAM MEETING TEN:
POKER FACE

> *"But you can't escape it—there is something wild in the heart of every man."*
> ~John Eldredge

What did you take away from last week's study and daily readings? What are you still processing? What challenged your current paradigm? What inspired you to grow as a man? Who can tell us what "poker face" means? How is the poker face advantageous in cards? In life?

How do people hide behind a poker face at work, church, or social gatherings? Is it possible for a man to lose himself over time behind his poker face façade?

"A tell in poker is a change in a player's behavior or demeanor that is claimed by some to give clues to that player's assessment of their hand. A player gains an advantage if they observe and understand the meaning of another player's tell, particularly if the tell is unconscious and reliable. Sometimes a player may fake a tell, hoping to induce their opponents to make poor judgments in response to the false tell. More often, people try to avoid giving out a tell, by maintaining a poker face regardless of how strong or weak their hand is."
~Wikipedia

What are some "tells" into a man's heart? Is there a way to see beyond his poker face and into his heart? What reveals the inner workings of a man?
Jeremiah 17:9 and 1 Corinthians 2:11

107

TEAM MEETING AT A GLANCE

- Opening Prayer, Weekly Announcements
- Personal and Victory Stories
- Each man will share his story—one man per week until all men have shared.
- After all men have shared their personal story, allow time each week for them to share victory stories.
- Weekly Study Closing Prayer
- Closing Prayer

"As water reflects a face, so a man's heart reflects the man."
Proverbs 27:19

Put Proverbs 27:19b, "so one's life reflects the heart" in your own words. How would you rewrite this? What does it mean?

"There are several suggestions as to the meaning of this proverb. First, the simplest way to take the verse is to say that, 'as clear water gives a reflection of the face, so the heart reflects the true nature of the man'.

Second, another suggestion is, 'through the observation of another that a man can know himself'. The point seems to be that it is through looking at our heart attitudes that we come to true self-awareness."
Expositor's Bible Commentary

What do you think about Adam Clarke's comment of Proverbs 27:19? Do you agree? Explain

"As a man sees his face perfectly reflected by the water, when looking into it; so the wise and penetrating man sees generally what is in the heart of another by considering the general tenor of his words and actions."
~Adam Clarke's Commentary

We understand the inside based on what we see and hear on the outside. Our words reflect our heart. Our public life gives us some insight into our private.
Matthew 12:33-37, 15:18-20, and James 3:1-12

> *"Actions speak louder than words, but not so nearly as often."*
> ~Mark Twain

Your outside reflects your inside. Your actions reflect your values. Your life reflects your heart. It isn't that people are judgmental. It's that they naturally fill in the blanks of your story based on what they see and hear.

"Esse quam videri."
To be, rather than to appear

If a reporter followed you for a month and interviewed those closest to you, what would they report that you value the most? If the man next to you did an extensive search through your cell phone, what would he say you value most?

> *"Discernment turns to judgment when you ask, 'Why?'"*
> ~Chuck Swindoll

What shocking inconsistencies might they uncover about the things you say you value versus what your life reflects? How is your life a contradiction to who you think you are? Where are you out of alignment with the man you claim to be?

Apathy hides behind the poker face of words, but values are manifest through action. People say, "Don't judge me?" How do we reconcile Jesus' words in Matthew 7:1-5 with those in Matthew 7:15-20? Is this a contradiction? What is Jesus telling us?

How do you balance discernment when transitioning from a poker face to a face-sharpening relationship?
Ephesians 4:14-16 and 25-32

> *"Let the world feel the weight of who I am, and let them deal with it."*
> John Eldredge
> *Wild at Heart*

Are you accurately reflecting your heart to the world?

Break into groups of three or four.

Where can you improve at reflecting the weight of your true self to the world?

Take a moment today and pray for each other.

> *"Life needs a man to be fierce—and fiercely devoted."*
> John Eldredge

STUDY NOTES

For the next five days, read the following entries from our **The Field Guide: A Bathroom Book for Men.**

We hope they challenge and encourage you to get in the great Arena for God. See you on the Arena Floor!

RUFFLED FEATHERS

Therefore, since we have such a hope, we are very bold.
2 Corinthians 3:12

I had the incredible privilege of calling in the Tom Turkey that is proudly displayed in my son Darby's room. It was his first. I'll never forget the moments before the shot as a hen, no more than three feet away, clucked uncontrollably as her two boyfriends strutted towards us with tail feathers fully fanned.

It was a brilliant display of glory.

Men are made to display God's glory. Glory is simply making something known that was previously hidden. It's putting something on display.

A man glorifies his God by living in bold obedience that proudly shouts, "May I never boast except in the cross of our Lord Jesus Christ, through which the world has been crucified to me, and I to the world" (Galatians 6:14).

Men however, tamed by a neutered culture that frowns upon biblical masculinity, are often tempted to fear this kind of display. Regardless, they shouldn't shrink back from living in the full glory of how they were created by God.

True manhood lives to glorify the King. You will ruffle feathers when you reclaim your rightful place from those who don't understand biblical masculinity.

God wants to put His men on display. God begins with men willing to fan their feathers, and ruffle others, in order to bring Him glory. Let those you love the most know of your "hope in Christ" even if it may ruffle some feathers. Stop fearing the glory.

Don't put your light under a bowl (Matthew 5:14-15). Keep your big God out of culture's small box. Put yourself on display as you live to glorify Him to the world.

THE INDICATOR

After they prayed, the place where they were meeting was shaken. And they were all filled with the Holy Spirit and spoke the word of God boldly.
Acts 4:31

Anyone who has played sports is familiar with signs. Signs are codes used to communicate strategy to your team with the opposition being none the wiser. Whether it's as simple as a number of fingers held high, code names, or human charades, signs are a critical aspect of communicating in sports.

The indicator is one tool coaches use to conceal signs. The indicator is a sign given to activate live signs. All signs are dummy calls until the indicator is given. In baseball, for example, if the indicator is a touch to the ear and the belt is the steal sign, the coach might touch his nose, elbow, wrist, and ear (the indicator), and then back to the belt to activate the live steal.

What's an indicator that a man is full of the Holy Spirit? How can you tell if he's all-in for God? For example, Galatians 5:22-23 is a place we find nine indicators of the Holy Spirit. We also see one in today's passage. This indicator is boldness— specifically, boldness in proclaiming the Word of God.

In Acts 4:33 we see that "with great power, the apostles were given witness to the resurrection of the Lord Jesus." Boldness isn't just proclaiming God's truth with authority, but living it confidently. Boldness cannot be hidden. It must be seen and heard.

When Jesus said, "Let your light shine before others, that they may see your good deeds and glorify your Father in Heaven" (Matthew 5:16), he was telling his followers to live out loud. Live boldly!

Let the world see and realize that you're all-in for Him.

DISEASE OF KINGS

…according to my earnest expectation and hope, that I will not be put to shame in anything, but that with all boldness, Christ will even now, as always, be exalted in my body, whether by life or by death.
Philippians 1:20 (NASB)

After an annual physical exam and blood work, my doctor said I had borderline high blood pressure, sugar, and high uric acid levels. I was told that the high uric acid levels made me a prime candidate for gout. I thought gout was something you put between tiles until now (nope, that's called grout).

But I was informed that gout, known as King's Disease, results from an over indulgence of meat, alcohol, or both. Since alcohol isn't an issue, I had to deal with my carnivorous lifestyle.

In medieval times, only the rich could regularly afford meat and alcohol. Now both are at the disposal of most Americans. We live in a time of Kings—fat, slow, and soft.

In today's passage Paul writes to the Philippian church while in prison. This epistle, along with Ephesians, Colossians, and Philemon, are called the Prison Epistles, since

Paul was incarcerated when he wrote them.

As Paul penned the words "with all boldness, Christ shall even now, as always be exalted in my body, whether by life or by death," he had to be thinking about his imminent death.

Men in America don't have to face martyrdom for our faith, yet we destroy our bodies with constant overdoses of high fructose corn syrup, hydrogenated oils, and processed foods. We've become a nation of gluttons. It's a daily battle to not be numbered among them.

What do we do? Will we continue down the dark path of gluttony, or repent and change our lifestyle? Get a grip on your gluttonous behavior before you have to be medicated because of it.

COACH CALMES

We were under great pressure, far beyond our ability to endure, so that we despaired even of life.
2 Corinthians 1:8

Somebody must have told Coach Calmes I was coming for my first day of weight training. As I rounded the corner to the weight room his voice echoed off the hallway, "Where's that mullet, Ramos! I want a piece of him, now!"

I never had a mullet haircut and to this day I don't know what he meant. But it didn't matter. He could say whatever he wanted. At six feet tall and weighing four hundred fifty pounds, my black strength training coach looked like a giant Hershey's Kiss.

The leg work out on that memorable day would be called abusive by today's standards. For a week I was too sore to stand upright. I literally walked the halls like an ape man. Years later, pushing through Coach Calmes' strenuous workouts helped me endure when pain begged to quit. I'm grateful to a man who was willing to challenge far beyond my limits.

Paul knew what it was like to push beyond his normal limits as well. He wrote today's Bible verse, "We were burdened excessively, beyond our strength" (NASB). Working within our limits is an excuse for mediocrity. Our limits contain what we can become with God's help. Staying within our limits removes the God component for those who ruthlessly trust Him. Paul knew this.

God calls our name from the halls. He calls us to greatness. But we hesitate, often ignoring Him until we're at the end of our rope. Instead, God meets us outside of our margins — beyond our reasonable limits.

It's at the end of our rope where we have no other choice but to trust God for a miracle, tie a knot and hold on. Don't hesitate when you hear Him calling. Act on what God puts on your heart.

Go beyond your limits for once.

OFFICE RULES

I heard a story about an irate church member who barged into the church office screaming obscenities at the unsuspecting church secretary. Scared for her life, she sat petrified in her chair as the angry parishioner towered over her, spitting out his vicious words.

Later she shared her story and I asked, "Where was the pastor? Wasn't his office a few feet from your desk?"

"He never came out." Her tone said it all. She'd lost respect for the man she once admired. He failed to stand in the gap for her. Ironically, the man was angry with the pastor and wanted to make an appointment with him! The pastor's cowardice forced the secretary into the potentially harmful situation. Stories like this remove the wonder behind why the modern church is so effeminate.

This passage is tough for me to wrap my American arms around. Peter, using Jesus as our example, suggests suffering should be a goal of discipleship because he was "an example for you to follow in his steps" (21).

One of the many roles of a man in following Jesus' example is to stand in the gap for the weak and powerless. If we need to fight, we should fight. If we need to defend, we should defend. If we need to suffer we should, "endure it patiently". At the very least, get out of your comfort zone and take the blows coming your way. Get uncomfortable for a change. Stand in the gap for someone in need.

Of course, you get no credit for being patient if you are beaten for doing wrong. But if you suffer for doing good and endure it patiently, God is pleased with you. To this you were called, because Christ suffered for you, leaving you an example that you should follow in his steps. ~ 1 Peter 2:20-21

NOW WHAT?!?

You just finished Book 1 of the Strong Men Study Series, defining the five essentials of manhood. You may be wondering, "Now what do I do?"

Thanks for asking. You have three options.
Option Uno: You can look for other resources for the men on your team.

Nah, we're just kidding. That's not an option.
Option Dos: You can move on to one of the other five books in the Strong Men Study Series until you've completed all five books, fifty of the team meetings, and 250 daily readings.

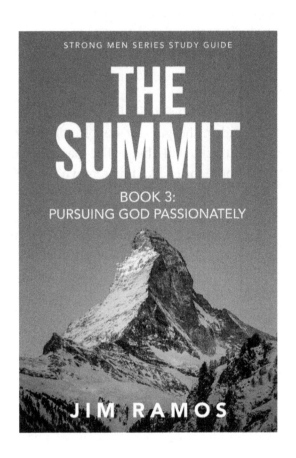

Those books are:

Book 1: The Trailhead: Protecting Integrity

Book 2: The Climb: Fighting Apathy

Book 3: The Summit: Pursuing God Passionately

Book 4: The Descent: Leading Courageously

Book 5: Trail's End: Finishing Strong

Option Tres: Visit our website (www.meninthearena.org) for other great resources to guide you to your best version of a man.

THE BATHROOM BOOK

Men are confused about what a man is. Is he a hunter, an extreme sports guy, or religious? Is he strong, a warrior, or a fighter? Is he a great athlete, rich, or famous?

Better yet, how does a male know when he's crossed into manhood? Is it chronological age? Is it anatomical? Is it when he is legally called a man? Is it becoming financially independent?

Where does a man learn about being a man? Is it from his dad, a coach, television, Google, The Bachelor, or possibly Chuck Norris?

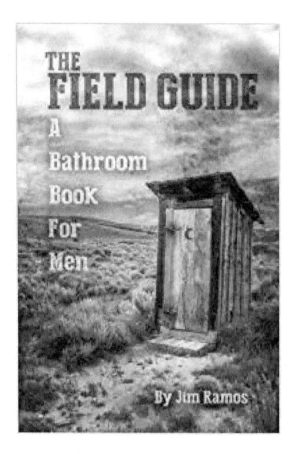

In the Field Guide: A Bathroom Book for Men, Jim Ramos uses his unique storytelling ability to tie masculine words in Scripture with everyday life. Day after inspiring day, the Field Guide weaves biblical themes of masculinity throughout the five essentials of manhood, "protecting integrity, fighting apathy, pursuing God passionately, leading courageously and finishing strong."

This book is a must-read for men. Place it at your bedside, in your office, man cave, or the back of your toilet. Use it as your favorite bathroom book. Read it daily. But be careful. The paper is no substitute for the real deal and will cut you! Only use it for reading!

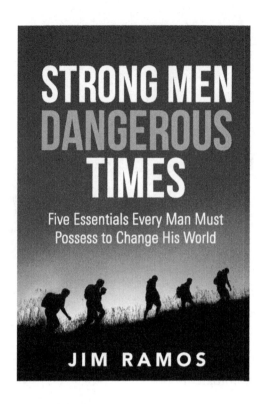

STRONG MEN DANGEROUS TIMES

Weldon M. Hardenbrook wrote, "Let's face it. It's extremely difficult for men to act like men when so much confusion exists about the definition of manhood. For most of human history, people knew what it meant to be a man. Now, at least in modern America, no one seems to know."

But men are conquerors. They seek the next hill to die on. They long for a mission to accomplish. They need a target to shoot at, but the sights have become blurry. Men are staring aimlessly through a dense fog of cultural ambiguity, and those they love are paying the price.

In his book Strong Men Dangerous Times: Five Essentials Every Man Must Possess to Change His World, Jim Ramos answers the question men have been asking for years, "What is a man?"

The simplicity of the book is brilliantly designed for the man who's too busy to read. It's short, to the point, and loaded with life application stories and will keep you on the edge of your seat!

Order your copy today.

ENLIST IN OUR ARMY

Facebook Forum

Join thousands of men from around the world in an open discussion on manhood! The Men in the Arena is a closed group for men only. It is the best free resource for men to discuss what a man is and does. Get out of the anonymous bleachers and into the Arena today!

Weekly Equipping Blast

Visit our website and subscribe to our weekly Equipping Blast. This is not spam or advertising. It is our weekly effort to guide you towards your best version.

Podcast

Subscribe to the Men in the Arena Podcast and learn from the top authors and experts on manhood on the planet.

GLOSSARY

The Definition (aka Five Essentials or Man Card): The Men in the Arena definition of manhood is "protecting integrity, fighting apathy, pursuing God passionately, leading courageously, and finishing strong." These are the things a man does to keep his Man Card.

Dioko: The Greek word the Apostle Paul used in Philippians 3:12 and 14 for "press on" meaning to hunt, pursue, or chase. It's where our name for The Great Hunt for God originated before we changed it to Men in the Arena!

Equipping Blast: Our weekly email blast is sent to thousands of men around the world. It includes our blog, podcast links, training videos, and more! Sign up at meninthearena.org.

Fighting Apathy: The second of the five characteristics of manhood demanding that men fight against all cultural resistance threatening to pull them down. Failure to resist this friction over time becomes apathy or callousness. Matthew 13:13-15 defines "callousness" as a lack of feeling that results when we fail to fight against the things trying to push us down. The second book in the Strong Men Study Series: The Climb, is dedicated to this topic.

Financial Champion: Did you know Men in the Arena is a crowd-funded organization? Crowd-funded means we strategically partner with generous people like you to fund our ministry. Please consider joining our great team of financial champions by signing up as a monthly donor on our website.

Finishing Strong: This is the last of the five traits of manhood, imploring men to finish every day strong to finish life strong. Each day's strong finish compounded over time completes a strong life finish.

Finishing is not the same as finishing strong. Please refer to 2 Timothy 4:6-7. The fifth book in the Strong Men Study Series: The Trail's End is dedicated to this topic.

Guardrails: Imagine traveling on the narrow road Jesus spoke of in Matthew 7:13-14. Its borders are lined with guardrails meant to direct and protect you as you travel through life. Guardrails are walls or hedges a man builds around himself and those he loves. Deuteronomy 22:8 is a great reference for building guardrails.

Intergenerational: One of the core values of the Men in the Arena is to lock shields with men representing all generations and decades of life.

Leading Courageously: The fourth of five aspects of The Definition imploring a man to step up and assume the role as patriarch and spiritual leader of the household. The fourth book in the Strong Men Study Series: The Descent, is dedicated to this topic.

Protecting Integrity: The first and foundational component in the Man Card describing the man who is mature, complete, and unbroken. Integrity is the sum of all character traits fully formed in a man. The first book in the Strong Men Study Series: The Trailhead, is dedicated to this topic.

Pursuing God Passionately: The third and climactic component of the Man Card. It's our adamant belief that no man can achieve his original design without radical obedience and relentless pursuit of his Creator and King. The third book in the Strong Men Study Series: The Summit, is dedicated to this topic.

Tag Line: We say it all the time. "When a man gets it - everyone wins!!"

Team Meeting: The weekly gathering of the Men in the Arena. Team meetings are designed to be no more than one hour in length and set to meet at the same time and place each week at the discretion of the team captains.

Vision: Our vision is simply trusting Jesus Christ to build an army of Men in the Arena, who are becoming their best version in Christ, and changing their world (because when a man gets it - everyone wins!).

COACHING TIPS

This Coaching Tips section is designed to help both new and seasoned Team Captains.

It offers helpful hints we've discovered in our years of running small groups with men.

Our one request is that you don't veer off course and go rogue with your team meetings. Our coaching tips are tried and true.

Feel free to add your personal style but avoid making it up as you go. We've been there—done that— and want to spare you the humiliation! Good hunting.

Big brother is watching: Your guys are watching you. They're watching how you live, love, serve, and run all team meetings.
Be an example.

Bring your A-Game: Bring your A-Game to the team meetings. Know who will and will not be present. Come prepared with notes in your workbook. If you have a co-captain, make sure you're on the same page. Men know when you come unprepared. This sends the wrong message.

Dynamics: How your team members are positioned in the room is crucial. The men need to sit at eye level and equidistant from the center of an eight-foot (maximum) diameter circle. If your circle, or any man, is further than four feet from center, your discussions will be greatly hindered.

Finger on the pulse: Your team will take on a unique identity. The morale of the men is at different levels, and group dynamics change constantly. What is the heartbeat of your men? Who's been missing? Who seems disengaged? Are you connecting with your co-captain(s)? What does your team need this week?

Floor Stare: Try this the next time you ask a question. Stare at the floor or at your workbook until guys begin to answer. Let them deal with the awkward silence and figure out an answer on their own.

Half Full Glass: Transforming lives is a journey. It's an investment into the lives of imperfect men. Even though these books are broken into ten-week bricks, our goal is to make a long-term investment in the transformational process.

But life is tough, and people are messy. When you lead your team, make sure to be positive. The negative will be easier to spot but be careful to acknowledge more positive than negative. It will pay dividends in the end.

Preparation is Key: Come prepared and ready to lead your team each week. The men on your team are watching you. They see the scribbled pages of preparation within the margins of The Man Card Series pages.

They also notice the blank pages when you come unprepared. Don't wing it and fling it. Bring your own thoughts and ideas to the table at every team meeting.

NEW TEAM LAUNCH STEPS

The Launch Steps are a tool to help Captains start a successful team.

Launch Step One: Co-Captain

Although it is not mandatory that you do this to launch a team, we highly recommend that you have another man to lock shields with through this process. There will be times you can't make it to the group, and it's good to know that someone has your back.

Besides recruiting team members, leaders often confess that finding their co-captain was the most challenging step in launching a new team. If you already have your co-captain, great job!

If you're struggling to find a co-captain, don't be discouraged. It's normal! When you approach a potential co-captain, and he has questions about the Men in the Arena and what you're asking him to do, send him to our website (www.meninthearena.org).

There, he can join our online forum, subscribe to our Equipping Blast, and receive all the information about Men in the Arena he needs to feel confident. Now you're ready to take on Launch Step Two.

Launch Step Two: Hit List

Hopefully, you were able to recruit a co-captain. If so, congratulations! Now it's time to put together your team. That's what building the Hit List is all about. Did you know that Jesus recruited a larger group of disciples before he chose the Twelve? Check it out:

"One of those days, Jesus went out to a mountainside to pray, and spent the night praying to God. When morning came, he called his disciples to him and chose twelve of them, whom he also designated apostles: Simon (whom he named Peter), his brother Andrew, James, John, Philip, Bartholomew, Matthew, Thomas, James, son of Alphaeus, Simon who was called the Zealot, Judas, son of James, and Judas Iscariot, who became a traitor."
Luke 6:12-16

With your co-captain, create two Hit Lists of at least 10-15 potential recruits—yours and his. Commit your Hit List to prayer, asking God to direct you through the process.

Once both lists have been compiled, pray over them, and decide who will receive a formal "call" (Launch Step Three) to be on your team. Some Team Captains invite all the men on their Hit Lists, while others are more selective. This is personal preference. Some Captains struggle to recruit enough men for their team. Others have to cut their Hit List down. Team size should range from a minimum of six to fourteen members maximum.

If possible, create an intergenerational team of men ranging throughout multiple decades of life. Once the Hit List is created, move on to Launch Step Three.

Launch Step Three: Call
Before you call each man, make sure you have the set time, date, and place of your first meeting—the Team Launch. This is important: you and your co-captain set the meeting day, time, and place, then tell the men. Don't ask the men what they prefer.

Make a decision before inviting men to join your team. Captains that try to please everyone on this issue lose. Some men won't be able to join your team simply because of your meeting times. That's normal, and you must be okay with it.

Once verbal commitments are made, move on to Launch Step Four.

Launch Step Four: Team List
How Captains communicate with their teams is partly what separates the good teams from the great ones. The Team List will be used on the Buy-In (Launch Step Six) and must include: Name (and wife's name), e-mail (and wife's e-mail), and cell phone number. The sooner an e-mail and text group are created, the more effective your team will be.

Use the Team List to remind the men about your weekly meetings. This acts as a reminder and gives men a simple way to reply if they can't make it that week.

We recommend putting together a calendar of key events for your team. Include your launch day, time, and place of weekly meeting, Team Potluck (Launch Step Five), and other important dates such as birthdays, important anniversaries, and regular social gatherings.

Launch Step Five: Team Potluck

You're almost there! You only have a few more steps until your Team Launch! Great job! We can't overemphasize the importance of the Team Potluck, especially for the married men. Use your Team List to communicate the time, date, and location of the Team Potluck.

Give your potential team at least three weeks' notice to save the date and communicate with their wives (Who should also be included in the email). We have found that the wives are usually the ones who manage the family calendar.

You should also invite the pastor who oversees small groups at your church. Have him pray for the meal and say a few words about the value of men in God's agenda.

Your goal is 100% attendance of those invited. One Team Captain confessed that he opted out of the potluck to hurry the process, and it was a monumental mistake.

The goal of the Team Potluck is to get total buy-in from the wives and have all questions answered. If the wife is in, the man is in. Trust us! We've seen it over and over. Attendance by the wives is critical for the success of Team Potluck.

Team Potluck Sample Agenda
- Dinner Responsibilities
- Captains supply the drinks and dessert
- Host home supplies dinnerware
- A-M Main Dish
- N-Z Salad (or dessert)

Sample Agenda (make it better)
- Fellowship
- Food (remember to pray before eating!)
- Captain and wife introductions
- Team member and wife introductions
- Review Team Launch information (day, time, and place), commitment level (75% attendance), and other pertinent information
- Explain the Buy-In (Launch Step Six)
- Q and A
- Pray for the group

Team Captain Commission: We believe in partnership with the local church and highly encourage Team Captains to get commissioned by a pastor or spiritual leader. If at all possible, get commissioned during the worship service at the church you attend. If not, the potluck is an appropriate option.
Fellowship

Launch Step Six: Buy-In
You can almost taste your Team Launch at his point. We're as excited as you to see lives transformed through your team!

All that's left is to order the books. Attrition will most likely claim some of the men, but we have found that the more the men buy in, the more committed they will be.
You can either buy the resources yourself, and the men reimburse you or send them directly to www.meninthearena.org and purchase the curriculum themselves.

Launch Step Seven: Commission and Launch
We hinted at this in launch Step Five: Team Potluck. Did you know that in the New Testament, the Twelve Apostles, the Apostle Paul—and Jesus—were commissioned in ministry? Have you been commissioned?

If not, we highly recommend it as a model for spiritual leadership. We believe so much in the local church that we strongly urge all team captains to be commissioned by their pastor or spiritual leader. Make it a public display. Here are some elements of a commission.

- Ceremony or public worship service
- Anointing and/or laying on of hands
- Public words of affirmation
- Giving of gifts (optional)
- Witnesses
- Spiritual leader
- Predecessor
- The Holy Spirit

Launch Step Eight: Team Launch Meeting One

Today's the day you've been working so hard for—Congratulations! This is an informational meeting only. Do not plan on going through the curriculum. Rather, make sure all of the men have it. If you don't meet where food and drinks are served, make sure they are available. Your first meeting should be one hour long from your designated start time (start on time, end on time).

Below is a sample agenda.
- Fellowship over food and drinks (10 minutes)
- Opening Prayer
- Restate the purpose, expectations, meeting agenda. Make sure they have purchased their books. (5 minutes)
- Men share about their lives, what they expect to get from the group, and where they are in their spiritual journey (40 minutes)
- Encourage and inspire them with your personal vision for the team. Be sensitive to where each man is. Be careful not to push too hard too fast. (5 minutes)
- Closing Prayer

Thank you so much for getting out of the anonymous bleachers and into the Arena! We are pumped to partner with you on your new adventure!

ABOUT JIM RAMOS

Thank you for taking your precious time to work through this book. I am honored and hope it inspired you on your journey towards the best you.

Lets lock arms on our journey. You can follow my journey on Facebook, Twitter, or Instagram @jimwramos.

I've been married to my best friend Shanna since 1992. She's the most important person in my life and my best friend. We love drinking coffee, traveling to tropical places, and eating out with friends.

I'm an avid book reader, enjoy fitness in the great outdoors, but my real passion is hunting. My sons are my hunting partners, along with a select few guys.

I love hanging out with men over a cup of good coffee and learning their stories. You can learn more about my story at meninthearena.org

Made in the USA
Las Vegas, NV
31 March 2022

46646100R00072